PREACHING THE ETERNITIES

The Warrack Lectures

PREACHING THE ETERNITIES

HAMISH C. MACKENZIE

EDINBURGH
The Saint Andrew Press

Published in 1963
by The Saint Andrew Press
at 121 George Street, Edinburgh, 2
and printed in Scotland by
The Tweeddale Press Ltd., Selkirk

* * *

FOREWORD

In that passionate day when the blood of the Covenanters ran fresh on the moorland, the Scottish Pulpit was apt to deal heatedly, and too exclusively, with current events. Almost alone among the ministers, Robert Leighton refused to countenance such work. Others, resenting this, asked him why he did not 'preach up the times'? 'Who does?' he enquired. 'We all do' was the reply. 'Then,' answered Leighton, 'if all of you are busy preaching up the times, you may forgive one poor brother for preaching up Christ Jesus and His eternity.'

ACKNOWLEDGMENTS

I WISH to thank the Committee in charge of the Warrack Lectureship for having honoured me with their confidence.

I am also indebted to the Principal and Staff of Christ's College, Aberdeen, and of Trinity College, Glasgow, who (early in 1962) contrived to find room for a Warrack Lecturer in their already crowded academic year. The hospitality which I received from them brings back the happiest memories. To the students and Christian friends who furnished me with such a stimulating body of hearers I am also most grateful.

Then perhaps I may be allowed to say how much I owe to the two splendid congregations of the Church which I have had the good fortune to serve—first at Bridge of Allan, and now for the major portion of my life at Giffnock. Almost everything I know about preaching I have learned from their friendship, patience, magnanimity and unfailing heart-leap to the Gospel cry.

Finally, I should like to pay tribute to my dear wife not only for some literary guidance and many helpful insights into evangelical religion but also for her constant and loving encouragement throughout all my ministry.

* * *

In the preparation of these Lectures for a wider public I have been greatly assisted by the expert knowledge of the Rev. Andrew McCosh and his very efficient colleagues at the Saint Andrew Press.

Manse of Orchardhill,
Giffnock.

September, 1963.

INTRODUCTION

As it is now many years since this Lectureship was founded one might suppose that there was little room left in it for originality. And to some extent that is the case. Why then attempt to say anything fresh about pulpit work? For exactly the same reason that we listen to familiar music. Every conductor of an oratorio uses the standard score, but each makes it yield a different result. The novelty lies not in the material but in the presentation. So any benefit the reader may derive from these lectures will issue much less from their formal teaching than from the author's own personal point of view. Therefore no excuse is required for traversing familiar ground except to say that what now follows is not, of course, a system of general validity but only a few familiar canons from one man's way of work. And if the truth were told, perhaps they indicate an ideal toward which he has striven rather than the reality which he has with any consistence achieved.

CONTENTS

I

CENTRALISE THE PULPIT!

SCRIPTURE holds that in the day of God ' our young men shall see visions.' Youth is the time for gazing into the landscapes of tomorrow. So when a man has answered the call to the Holy Ministry, he should *want* to preach, to broadcast the Good News to the multitude. The pulpit is the place in which he is going to spend his greatest hours. . . .

It was certainly in terms like these that theological students of a former day conceived the ministerial life. They thought of the work to which they were committed as predominantly a matter of preaching. That, as they understood it, was the main business of the Reformed Church. And history seemed to homologate their view. For hundreds of years Public Worship in Scotland had centred round the proclamation of the Word of God. As at Calvin's Geneva, so also here in this country, the words ' Service ' and ' Sermon ' were inter-changeable. The one implied the other. Hence the first thing needed to make a fully-fledged church was ' supply of sermon.' Worshippers were spoken of as ' common hearers.' Prayer and praise were referred to as ' the preliminaries.' The congregation was said to ' sit under ' Mr So-and-So. Such language was used, not to minimise the spiritual value of man's offering to God, but simply because everything in the worship led up to the supreme act—the utterance of God's word to man.

Now this outlook, so characteristic of the thought-world of our forefathers, was by no means unknown in earlier times. Even as far back as the fourth century John Chrysostom could ask, 'Know you not how great a love of preaching at present possesses the souls of Christians?' But with the growing infamy of the Mediæval Church the appeal of the pulpit seems steadily to have diminished, until about the fifteenth century (we are told) 'The office of preaching as a general part of the Pastor's duty had largely fallen into abeyance.' So it was no wonder that the cleansing of the Lord's household should have been followed by an upsurge of desire for the living Word. This was indeed one of the characteristic marks of the whole Reforming movement. Sir David Lyndesay describes how ordinary folk, weary of the mumbo-jumbo of the Roman friars, hungered for honest preaching:

'Quho can not preche, a Preist sulde not be namit' he says. And suggests:

'That thair be given to na man bishopries,
Except they preich out throch thair diosies;
And ilk persone preich in his parochon. . . .'

That was in the sixteenth century. In the seventeenth preaching was still the one thing that Scotsmen demanded indifferently from curate or covenanter. In the eighteenth it was supplied for them in rich abundance by the 'Marrow men' and the Secession worthies. In the nineteenth it continued to be the glory of the Victorian pulpit—so much so that there has perhaps never been an age when so many great and distinguished men were to be found opening the word of God to crowded congregations every Sunday.

The church-goer of those days had been brought up on preaching. He had watched a long succession of men in gown and bands climbing the pulpit stair. He knew how the light would fall on their faces. With expectation he waited for their opening word. Every Service was an adventure. And while there were times when some crudity in the herald made it hard to listen with profit, there were other occasions—many of them—when the folk in the pews heard the trumpets of God and saw the shekinah-glory. Therefore it was the habit of many devout persons who lived in the city to go on Sabbath evenings to some favourite church where (even at the discomfort of standing for an hour in the queue) they could enjoy the privilege of hearing a well-known man of God speak to their soul. Doubtless there was an element of hero-worship in it. And perhaps they were not always free from the vice of sermon-tasting. But for the most part they really hungered after God. And they found in listening to such pulpit giants an experience which often enough transformed their whole existence.

These days have vanished. They ceased, roughly speaking, with the First World War. True, even in the twentieth century we are not without some very gifted preachers. And there are perhaps more churches than the uninstructed think which can still show a crowded congregation. But the world in which every modern ministry is being exercised has changed. New forces are at work. Radio has popularised group-discussion and five-minute epilogues. Notice-boards advertise 'Cinema Services.' There is a fresh emphasis on the 'house-church.' Around many a charge has grown up a host of parasitic clubs and societies which threaten to strangle it. Certain quarters reveal a trend toward ecclesiasticism, formalised worship, sacramentarian theories, religious labour-projects, and a semi-monastic ideal strangely out of keeping with our Reformed heritage.

One must of course expect some measure of change in the familiar scene as time goes by. And it need cause no perturbation as long as it does not touch the fundamentals. But that is the rub. The official Church is now re-shaping her basic economy, as it were, to fit the new state of things. And the chief evidence is that preaching no longer comes first. Indeed it is often spoken of now —and, alas, chiefly by ministers themselves—in a tone of near-contempt. To describe anyone as a 'popular preacher' is almost to accuse him of being a cheap fellow engaged in huckstering the Gospel. True, congregations on the whole are still sound. The inarticulate mass of the people have a native instinct that makes them want good sermons. But they find it hard to resist the trend of the age. And they are very much in the hands of those whose business it is to take charge of their ecclesiastical destiny. So when constantly told by church representatives and church publications that preaching is the last thing to think of, they ultimately begin to want other things very much more—an attractive way with youth, organising ability, power of leadership, scholastic distinction, a flair for ceremonial. These of course are useful gifts and accomplishments. No believer could possibly have anything against them. There has always been a great variety in God's household. It is clear that the Church can be served, and served admirably, along such lines. Yet, with every desire to accord them their due, one must point out that in the last analysis they are secondary and subordinate. That is why it is distressing to find that they are now being allowed to usurp a place in the Church's own view of her mission to which they are certainly not entitled.

The result is that preaching has lost its primacy—a fact declared by the modern habit of removing the pulpit to an insignificant side-position. Folk still come to the Sunday Services; but speaking generally their reason is not, above all else, to 'hear the Word of God.' They are encouraged by the whole spirit of the time to have other motives. Excellent however as these may be, they are no substitute for the original. It is absolutely necessary for the members of a New Testament church to concentrate on the preaching. 'Faith cometh by hearing, and hearing by the Word of God.' When this is relegated to a secondary place, it has a baneful effect not only on congregations but even more upon their ministers. To preach with his whole soul a man must face an expectant people. Judged by purely technical standards, sermons today are probably as well constructed as in any previous age. But their effect is far from comparable with their craftsmanship. How many parishes are there left in Scotland where the pulpit utterance is still the great event of the week?—where it is recalled, examined, discussed, ingested, and applied to the hearer's walk and conversation.

No; the old leisurely ways are gone. Science has transformed our common existence. Where is the pulpit sandglass now? Men and women have wider interests and less patience than their forefathers. Ours is not the only voice to which they feel obliged to listen. The modern world, like Prospero's isle, is 'full of noises.' A dozen different broadcasters compete for every metre of the wave-band. So the sermon tends to be but one of many allocutions addressed to the public. And, besides, the ears on which it falls are no longer those of persons deeply troubled by the uncertainty of life. Folk may have their own worries—but not that. Two hundred years ago a poor harvest might involve semi-starvation for the whole countryside. Pain had to be borne because there was often neither drug nor surgery to relieve it. Many a married pair in the course of establishing a family paid six or seven heart-broken visits to the graveyard. And therefore eternity crowded in upon their horizons. They were conscious of their need for divine help in a sense in which few understand it now. Citizens of the Welfare State are so cushioned against calamity that they can avoid thinking even about their latter end.

All these changes have robbed the pulpit of some of its effectiveness. And yet none of them really constitute a lasting hindrance. We could have adapted our methods to the new day but for treachery on the part of the Church herself. The real enemy is within. This generation has lost faith in the ministry of the Word. Reversing the classic order, we place it not among the *necessities* but only among the *benefits* of the Church. So many a man who in these days goes up to the bookboard on a Sabbath morning is reduced to impotence before he starts. He may have workmanlike notes in his sermon-folio. He may rightly divide the scripture and with genuine skill expound and illustrate it. His words may be well-pleasing to the bulk of his auditory. But the likelihood is that they will have small religious effect. They will win no souls, nor even do much to nourish those that are already won, because the whole business—intelligent and acceptable as it is—lacks certain vital qualities without which no miracles of grace are ever wrought. And these are absent for the simple reason that quite apart from the shortcomings of his people, the man himself does not wholeheartedly believe in a number of truths that were taken for granted by his forefathers. . . .

For example, that he has authority to speak. Of course the Church has licensed him. But it is one thing to have official warrant; it is quite another to enjoy that inward assurance which substantiates the utterance of all who hold forth in God's name. For various reasons (some of which we shall examine by and by) many a modern preacher has acquired an apologetic approach to his ministry. He looks on words as rather feeble weapons. He hesitates to dogmatise before cultured people who have no chance to answer back. After all, his is a pretty sheltered life compared with that so rumbustiously led by some of his hearers. And then the national Church herself does not help him to be any more confident than he is; for instead of crying triumphantly 'We are able!' she habitually speaks in a self-depreciatory tone about her character and achievements.

This hesitant attitude with its over-willingness to admit fault is due to lack of a proper sense of authority. Why should a man trouble to preach unless he knows that he is commissioned to do so? This is not a private opinion that comes forth from his lips. It is the Word of God. In, through, and behind it, the listening ear will detect the accents of the Almighty. As God said to Ezekiel, 'I do send thee unto them; and thou shalt say unto them, "Thus saith the Lord."' It is as simple as that—not our proclamation, but His. Who is going to pay any serious attention to an uncertain trumpet? Why indeed should people be expected to do so? If the most we can say for the Church is that she is humbly willing to learn from her mistakes, and that she might some day have a certain amount of good advice to give, the doors might as well be shut for ever! We must speak with authority. That is the only justification for our work. The pulpit is still a throne. Once an individual realises that he has a right to be there, he takes command. Gone are the tentative ideas, the unfounded hopes, the apologetic conclusions. He has something to say; a strong clear word. Whether anyone will listen to it is no concern of his; but speak he must for his lips have been touched with the altar-flame.

Moreover, a man must believe that his preaching is intelligible, that it will actually be grasped and understood by his hearers. Naturally he should cultivate simple speech. But, more than that, he should have confidence in the transmissibility of his ideas. It is quite true that there are some audiences with whom we find it hard to be 'en rapport.' The world in which they habitually live is not ours. And yet as long as these folk enjoy a modicum of intelligence they are perfectly capable of apprehending enough of what we say to bring them face to face with God. Churchmen psychologise too much. And therefore a good deal of nonsense has been talked about 'the problem of communication,' as if the human race in modern days were somehow divided up into island groups, or even into an archipelago of solitary individuals, each cut off from all the others by virtue of an inherent inability to make himself known. To argue on these lines is to magnify an admitted and occasional difficulty until it becomes a general absurdity.

Of course preachers do, to some extent, use a specialised language. Words like 'grace,' 'justification,' 'atonement,' may be devoid of meaning for those who have little knowledge of the Bible. But there are plenty of other expressions which convey the substance of the Christian Faith and the realities of the moral life. 'What can be known about God,' says St Paul, ' is plain to men, because God has shown it to them. . . .' But ' they did not see fit to acknowledge God.' So much for the theory that a large part of this generation simply cannot guess what the Church is talking about. On the contrary, when the matter is clearly stated they apprehend it very well. They do not require that we should address them in some affected argot. Plain English is still good enough. We have been far too ready to accept sinners at their own valuation. Many a would-be intellectual, hinting at profundities of philosophic doubt, is just a bad boy running away from his Heavenly Father. And many a class-conscious trade-unionist, putting up an ideological smoke-screen is merely a waster trying to hide the guilt of his own sordid existence. There is no real difficulty in being understood—only in winning the allegiance of the heart after we have secretly convinced the head. So the preacher should speak boldly and forget about ' communication.' The people have ears to hear. Let them hear!

And we must believe in the relevancy of our message. It deals with things that are the vital concern of every human soul. Men are so created that they need divine help if they are to live a truly satisfying life. Every attempt to leave God out and go ahead by themselves is bound to meet with disappointment in the latter end. So religion is essential—not just a desirable extra but an absolute necessity. The trouble is that it does not always look like that. The information that Mr A. has just won thousands of pounds in a lottery grips the public mind. But the fact that Mr B. has had a wonderful experience of the grace of God—even though we were to noise it far and near—would rouse no comparable excitement. 'Spiritual things are spiritually discerned.' And so the values of the man-in-the-street tend to be grossly material. He inhabits a world which he thinks perfectly solid but which has often little relation with reality.

These are the folk to whom our message is directed. They need to listen to it. Salvation itself depends upon a faith-response. Why then should we attempt to justify our ministry? Let the preacher stand his ground and refuse to be jockeyed aside by the claim that other and more important voices should now address the multitude. There is no more important voice than ours. What we have to say touches life at the quick. Man does not live by bread alone, however large his portion of the loaf may be. God's Word is still the first essential. And the task of those to whom it is committed takes precedence over all others. We have the greatest of earthly callings; the one which makes the noblest contribution to human happiness both here and hereafter. Therefore we need no magical endowment to convince us that our job is indispensable. It is enough that God has opened our lips. When He made His only Son a preacher, surely He believed that men needed preaching, the right kind of preaching, more than anything else in the world.

We need a great revival of preaching. But it will come only when men are persuaded that this is in very deed the first of all their labours. Jesus himself was in no doubt of that, as we see from the opening sentence of his ministry, ' The Lord hath anointed me to preach. . . .' And when, later on, he commissioned his disciples, he said, 'As ye go, preach. . . .' We just cannot have the Ministry at all—apart from a few specialised forms of it—on any other ground. Admittedly, for the teaching or pastoral office God sometimes sees fit to require a man's whole life; but the vast bulk of ministers are more likely to find their charge in the apostolic statement, ' He commanded us to preach unto the people.' This which is set forth in scripture has also been written into our confessional symbols. The earliest, and (as some hold) perhaps the best, of the Reformed group is of course the famous Scots Confession of 1560. Its authors say, ' The note therefore of the true Kirk of God we believe, confess, and avow to be, first, the true preaching of the Word of God. . . .' They then go on to speak of Sacraments, which come second; and Discipline, which comes third. But it is expressly laid down that the Sacraments must be linked with the Word, and that the Discipline must be found in the Word. So the Word is regulative for the others; and the true preaching of the Word is the dominant and typical mark of the Christian Ecclesia.

We do not of course suggest that unless a church puts preaching in the forefront it is necessarily devoid of grace. That would be patently absurd. It is not for us to limit the work of the Holy Spirit. Beautiful Christians can be found, as we all know, in every existing denomination.

The Church—however strangely altered from the New Testament pattern she may be—is nevertheless so full of riches that people can enjoy within her fellowship a genuinely abundant life, even though the sermons there may not receive the same emphasis as in a Bible-based ministry. The Word that stirs their faith is not in every instance mediated exclusively through the pulpit. Yet when that is allowed for, the fact remains that there is a divine norm for the Church. It should be a simple gathering of believers in which God speaks through a chosen ministry. Our forefathers had tried the other thing —the vast ecclesiastical empire with its ritual of sacrifice; and they were quite sure that that was contrary to the mind of our Lord. Granted that among all the different branches of His household on earth not one is perfect. Each has its own strength and weakness. But while maintaining a charitable outlook on our neighbours, we ought to give whole-hearted allegiance to our own communion. We of the Reformed Church believe that in the true Kirk the pulpit comes first. That is how we understand God's direction to us in scripture. We can find no authority for laying the emphasis elsewhere. The pulpit comes first. Not the communion table. Not the halls. Not the works of necessity and mercy. But the pulpit. The pulpit is central. The whole life of the congregation turns on the message God gives to us. Preaching first; all else that is helpful afterward. That is the right order. Thank God for the biblical insight with which our forefathers discerned it!

'True preaching'! That is what we need in every corner of the land. It does what nothing else can do. It is the divinely appointed method for drawing the human heart to its Maker. One thinks of that Communion week-end at Shotts away back in 1630 when John Livingston opened up a passage from Ezekiel by the space of two and a half hours, and was so graciously assisted in the latter part of his discourse that hundreds were converted. At Cambuslang in 1742 George Whitefield preached to immense crowds gathered on the hillside; and long years afterward the local minister testified that of those who had then accepted Christ at least four hundred were still standing. During the blessed awakening at Perth in 1840 William Burns one night addressed a packed congregation; and next forenoon the church became the rendezvous of several hundred people who had returned to seek guidance about the state of their soul. And if we look at our own day we must surely make mention of that young evangelist, reared in the traditional piety of North Carolina, who has probably seen more signs following his Gospel message than any other man in human history. The reason for this is clear. When a man preaches, he declares a living word. It therefore communicates life—and life is something that far outruns the bounds of language, or even of any particular personality. It rebukes, convicts, inspires. At one stroke it abolishes the cheap newspaperish world in which much of our speaking today is done, and brings us face to face with the holiness and majesty of God.

We in this generation have lost sight of that; and therefore many of our sermons are conceived in a non-religious atmosphere. One can almost guess by the flatness of the speech that they are ignorant of eternity. The resonance has faded. The undertones and overtones are gone. So we need to learn anew the possibilities of the medium with which we work. Preaching is a tremendous thing. There is nothing remotely comparable to it for changing human lives. It has revolutionised whole communities. Therefore the current disparagement of preaching falls like a blight on our land. Everyone who disbelieves in the ministry of the Word is exercising a pernicious influence upon others. What does he propose to put in its place? How else are men and women to be brought to God? There have been, admittedly, a few revivals (like that in Wales sixty years ago) which crept silently upon the Church as a result, so it would seem, of group devotion. But for the most part God has raised up a preacher, or a succession of preachers, to sway the multitude. The trouble is that if we ourselves have never been privileged to witness the folk bend like ripe corn in response to the moving of the Holy Spirit, we have no idea what the pulpit can do. Those who keep a steam-hammer to crack nuts may forget in the end that its original assignment was to forge propellor-shafts. The religious destiny of this island is, humanly speaking, in the hands of its preachers. It is the man who stands forth on the Lord's Day to speak for God who is the most likely channel for a divine outpouring.

To be a preacher of the type just indicated one must have a Call. 'No man taketh this honour unto himself.' The Ministry is not a job; it is a vocation. Blessed are they who have felt that from their earliest days, and who could echo the statement of the Apostle Paul, 'God . . . separated me from my mother's womb and called me by his grace . . . that I might preach. . . .' It is an inspiring thing to be aware with utter certainty that this is what one was born to do. But when this is not revealed to a man in childhood, he must wait until there is some later evidence. For a 'Call' he must have. It is not true that the requirements of the Church plus the possession of certain gifts form together a suitable substitute. As well might a random couple marry on some theoretic ground and expect love to follow. That was not how the Song of Songs came to be written. The Call is a 'thing-in-itself,' as unmistakable and ineluctable as our romantic destiny.

Of course people sometimes err. A few years ago a minor but well-known dignitary of the Church of England published a volume of memoirs. Discussing ordination, he said, 'In my own case, there were certain other callings which attracted me. With more money, I would have wished to become a barrister; with more brains, to try for the Indian Civil Service. Neither was really open to me . . . I am still haunted by the feeling that my decision to be ordained was based on very insufficient ground.' Precisely! Without the main motive, what could the results be but disappointing? There is always a certain number of men who for one reason or another find themselves at the feast without a wedding garment. They may be quite decent fellows who, after a while, realising the impossibility of their position, contract out. Or they may be so insensitive, such oafish creatures, as to go in happy ignorance of their solecism. Or they may even be rogues determined to exploit the Ministry for their own advantage. Do you wonder that as he passed the kirk door of one such, Murray McCheyne 'raised his hand with vehemence, as he spoke of the people left to perish under such an incumbent.' The genuine shepherd would give his life for the sheep. So if a man is in two minds about ordination, if he could possibly do anything else without breaking his heart, let him go while there is still time. The world holds many another field of service. The only valid reason for entering the Ministry is that one feels onself drawn into it by the hand of God.

It is the sense of call that authenticates a man's ministry. This is what gives him the right to stand up in church and address the people in God's name. He is not there for any private purpose but as the ambassador of the King of Kings. The Almighty is against such as take on this work at their own charges. These are the 'false shepherds.' He did not send them. They have climbed up into the pulpit by some back stair like an unwanted presentee. But the man whom God Himself has ordained knows that this is his legitimate environment. If anyone should ask (as the spies did of Micah's priest), 'Who brought thee hither? and what doest thou in this place?' he can give an immediate and conclusive answer. The Lord has chosen him. 'I thank God that of His grace He called me into this ministry,' said Samuel Chadwick. 'I have loved my job with a passionate and consuming love. I would rather preach than do anything else I know in this world.' That is the true tone and temper of those who have been summoned to act as a mouth-piece for the Most High.

And it is this that carries them through all the trials necessarily involved in such a life. Once a man quits the Divinity Hall he becomes immersed in cares and responsibilities. Little by little the morning glory fades. There is some natural waning of enthusiasm. He may experience financial hardship. Children can bring sorrow. As like as not, when he most needs it, some expected translation fails to materialise. Judas-work perhaps distresses the body of the faithful. He spends himself to the uttermost, yet showers of blessing tarry. So at last a day may come when, if it were not for his call, he might be tempted to seek an easier lot. But how can he even think of it as long as that fire burns in his bones? He is called; yielded up; the subject of a divine espousal. With his latest breath he must serve the Lord.

It is not that there is nothing else he could do. There may be several attractive alternatives open to him. But he is no more in a position to take advantage of these—honourable and rewarding as they are—than he is to commit bigamy. The eternal God has made him a man of one concern. He is exactly what the gracious tradition of the Southern States in America will have every

'Reverend' to be—a 'Preacher.' Not Mr This or Dr That; not Your Grace or Your Holiness; but simply 'Preacher'! 'Preacher'!—That is his badge; that is his dignity; that is the sign by which he is known among men. Preacher! And no preacher should do anything but preach. For preaching is a whole-time job. There is not one man in a thousand who can successfully combine it with something else—farming, for example; or journalism; or education; or salesmanship; or (in the regular absence of his working wife) domestic service. Even hobbies can be dangerous for a preacher. It never yet enhanced any man's power in the Gospel that he was frequently found amusing himself either in or out of doors.

This is not to advocate a puritanical otherworldliness. It is merely to say that for the true servant of God preaching comes first and must have his undivided loyalty. The 'two-purpose' gadget is generally a failure. It does neither job well. There is a Gaelic proverb, 'When we are seeking gold, let us be seeking gold; and when we are seeking bait, let us be seeking bait.' One thing at a time is sound psychology, and good religion. We cannot draw off fifty per cent (or even twenty per cent) of our mental and spiritual energies for some purpose unconnected with the Gospel, and then expect our message on the Sabbath to be such as the Holy Ghost is likely to use. The real reason for much pulpit inefficiency is that the would-be herald of God has been running around to dozens of needless engagements when he should have been in his study. preparing to preach. Let it be said again, that for every minister of the Reformed Church preaching comes first. The Bible declares it. Our subordinate standards record it. If anything else is holding up the Word of God then it must go. We have to learn to be almost fanatical about this. Satan loves those broad-minded folk who think preaching important, very important; but not primary. If he can keep a man from putting it first, he has that congregation safely in his keeping. The Devil is not afraid of general religious activity. What makes him tremble is the Word. How right Luther was when he said in 'Ein Feste Burg,' 'A word shall quickly slay him'—yes; God's Word!

Glorious indeed would it be if the ministers of the twentieth century believed that! One sometimes wishes there were a specially appointed angel who could take any man with a clerical collar aside and ask him lovingly, 'Brother, what comes first in your work for God? Are you a Preacher? Do you live to preach? Is it your absorbing interest night and day? Or is it something you would fain push into the background? If so, let me ask you a question—What would you think of a soldier who threw away his weapon and gave it out that the business of the Army was to make beds, keep fit, and to take some courses in Civil Engineering? Would you not say, "This man's values are confused. He must have been brain-washed by the enemy; for he has lost sight of what is implied in being a soldier."' At that point the angel could stop. He would at least have made his companion think. And the fellow badly needed to do that. There are not a few men of his type in the Ministry—honest enough souls but quite muddled. Sometimes they suspect that the greatest hindrance to the Kingdom of God is their own backsliding. In one way that does them credit; but they are wrong. Sin can be pardoned. What God can do nothing with is a reversal of values. We all recognise that when men call evil good, and good evil, they are finished. That is spiritual death. But what we do not so often realise is that when they put secondary things first, and the first second, they are in an almost equally hopeless condition. Yet that is what has happened in some measure today. The Church has left her first love. . . . Riding the morning swell off St Andrews, John Knox looked up from his galley-oar and saw the place where, as he said, 'God first called me to the dignity of a preacher.' We are his descendants. Ours is the same commission. To preach. Let us be then what we are called to be—preachers. Heaven ordains it. Hell fears it. Earth requires it. Our life, and the life of every congregation, hangs upon it. Let not only the City of Glasgow (which claims the motto) but all broad Scotland as well, 'flourish by the preaching of His Word and the praising of His Name.'

II

FINDING A MESSAGE

THE preacher is a Voice—' the voice of one crying.' He stands forth to deliver the Word of the Lord. This is the sole reason for his existence. All else concerning him may with advantage be wrapped in obscurity. The world is not helped by exposure of his private life. Doubtless he has to eat and drink. Somewhere, it may be, he shares the intimacies of an earthly home. But his great business is preaching. He lives to acquaint the world with God. In the solemn moment when he first learned that he was ordained to be a prophet of the Lord, heaven said to him ' Cry!' And he must cry, for the word is as a fire shut up in his bones. Whether or not anyone chooses to hear; whether the cost of such unburdening be public disapproval, ostracism, or even martyrdom—nevertheless he must cry. It is the mark of idols, says the Psalmist, that ' they speak not through their throat.' The true God makes Himself known by His utterance. He communicates with men—sometimes in words audible to them alone; more often by using heralds and ambassadors. These chosen servants speak out what God desires His people to know. And in the very midst of their forth-telling the listener is conscious of that which comes from the mouth of the Almighty.

What is it that we are summoned to declare? There is but one reply, ' The whole counsel of God ' (Acts 20, 27).

Yet it has never been easy to state the precise content of the message. Like most big things it refuses to exhaust itself in a single simple formula. Three main elements are, however, involved. . . .

First, God speaks to us through the revelation given in Hebrew history. It is therefore an unwarranted curtailment of the message to limit it to certain dominical events. Christ did not begin his work only with his earthly life. 'The scriptures,' he said, 'are they which testify of me.' In other words, he was being proclaimed long before he was born. The Jewish Church had in its hands the whole of the Old Testament with its messianic predictions and its many sidelights on the coming Lord. So the Gospel was not quite unheard-of, a sheer novelty published throughout the world only after Pentecost. From as far back as the earliest stirrings of the chosen race it had in some measure been sounded forth and recognised for what it was. The prophets had uttered it. And also the Psalmists, in those golden verses which even yet carry the burden of so much Christian prayer. Jesus himself preached it in Galilee, taking his text from the 'good tidings' of Isaiah. The author of Hebrews speaks of it as having been familiar to the tribesmen who left Egypt under the leadership of Moses. Paul affirms in Romans that it was the very rejection of this age-old 'Gospel' by his fellow-Jews which brought blessing to the Gentiles.

Then, secondly, God speaks to us through the revelation given in the Incarnation. To gaze at Jesus' earthly walk in Galilee is to realise that everything about our Lord is full of converting power. There never was in all the ages of the world a personality so calculated to strike the observer dumb with awe. His lightest word, his least-considered acts, have a quality of moral grandeur that needs heaven to explain them. It is safe to say that any honest enquirer who studies the life recorded by the four Evangelists will emerge from it humbled and amazed. And this is specially true of the final scene upon the Cross. At Calvary we find the answer to the dilemma, 'How can wickedness be pardoned without undermining the holiness of God?' That required an atonement of cosmic outreach. Hence these scriptures: 'He was sacrificed for us'; 'He was delivered for our offences'; 'He bore our sins in his own body'; 'The Lord hath laid on him the iniquity of us all'; 'He was made to be sin for us who knew no sin'; 'He loved me, and gave himself for me.' There may be other activities involved in reconciling men to God, but this substitutionary element is at the very heart of it.

> Bearing shame and scoffing rude,
> In my place condemned He stood,
> Sealed my pardon with His blood:
> Hallelujah! what a Saviour!

On this infinitely precious doctrine a man may rest his soul, because it is true, and because it cannot be taken out of the Bible without destroying the whole revelation.

Then, thirdly, God speaks to us through the revelation given in Christian morality. Jesus laid it down that even in the post-Resurrection age the Holy Spirit would continue his labours. 'He shall glorify me . . . for he shall receive of mine, and show it unto you.' Here we are concerned with the discipline of the believer's life and the sanctifying of his conduct. Now there have always been those in the Church who made a sharp distinction between Law and Gospel, much to the detriment of the former; as if one could not speak on moral subjects without abandoning the whole business of salvation. But that is a false antithesis. The new life in Christ involves not only joyous liberty but also hard and unremitting effort. Every congregation needs a word from time to time on such matters as Honesty, Purity, Self-control, Church-Going, Liberality, Unworldliness, the Keeping of Vows, the Training of Children, and so forth. Any true Gospel must contain an element of moral challenge. For God is a holy God. He passionately desires that men and women should behave themselves according to His commandments. Therefore souls have to be searched. Hidden things need to be brought to judgment. When people grow careless they must be made to hear the thunders of Sinai and to feel the hand of the Almighty hurling them to the ground. It is no pleasant job. Few audiences like this sort of thing. And we ourselves would in most cases prefer (as someone has said) 'to leave the prophet's blood-stained mantle hanging in the vestry.' But it has to be done. It can be done with tenderness. And the doing of it is an essential part of a faithful and comprehensive ministry.

The preacher then has something quite specific to say. It need not be confined to any one particular aspect of the Gospel. His business is to expound the many-sided goodness of God. But chiefly he will rejoice in proclaiming 'Jesus Christ and him crucified.' The Cross-note will seldom be absent from his utterance. And those who hear this message in all its varied grandeur will recognise its supernatural quality. The whole 'feel' of the thing will be authoritative, otherworldly, divine. This is what one often misses in the Church today. The sermon tends to be only a series of insights and observations by a well-meaning religionist. These may be interesting enough; and even helpful after a sort. But they don't strike us as a communication from on high. The man speaks for himself. This is what *he* thinks about God. The hearers get 'views instead of news.' But that is surely an altogether inadequate reason for his being there. One such minister was very fond of using the sentence, 'We are entitled to suppose . . . ,' until finally a disgusted woman who yearned for firmer standing-ground burst out, 'We are not entitled to suppose anything!' She was justified. Supposition has no place in the Gospel. It is the preacher's charge to bring his people a certainty. He is to tell them, not what he thinks; but who God is, what God has done, and what God is now saying to their souls. Men need this 'word for living.' It must supplement the bread on their table if they are not to perish. So every week they are entitled to hear it—strong, clear, factual, objective, and assured.

To preach like this a man must do three things. *First, Accept the Bible as the Word of God and the Rule of Faith and Life*. His message comes, and can only come, from the Bible. To 'preach the Gospel' is to declare and expound the Word of God from the scriptures of the Old and New Testaments. We have no legitimate ground for going outside Holy Writ. A text is not a pretext on which to hang a number of private opinions. We must at least respect God's Book. On this head most of us will find ourselves in agreement. One does hear, of course, from time to time about a few individuals who make a habit of preaching from poets, novelists, the latest fad, or some casual incident; but in Scotland at least the bulk of ministers still stick to the Bible. Our texts rise out of the sacred page. Yet even so, there are to be found among us two strongly contrasting views of holy scripture. Of course even those who see things from the same angle would not all express themselves in exactly the same terms. Yet the existence of a deep-going distinction is clear.

That is not to say that all conservatives are necessarily Gospel preachers, and that those who take the liberalistic line are mere humanitarian idealists. Reality can seldom be parcelled out quite as neatly as that. Besides, we are never justified by our intellectual convictions alone. God can, and does, honour the ministry of men who (as we might think) are far from being sound even on the gravest issues. Hence the need for charity in making pronouncements about the worth of other people's religion. Nevertheless, we are obliged to support the truth as we have been given to know it. And therefore some of us would hold that the traditional understanding of the Bible as the Word of God written, fully inspired and absolutely trustworthy, is the only view which does justice to the claims of scripture, the teaching of our Lord, and the inherent necessities of the Evangel. Only with such a Book (and here, like William Penn, we say, 'I speak my experience')—only with such a Book do we find it possible to preach with power and see signs following.

The Bible is the very Word of God. That is what it claims for itself. 'The Spirit of the Lord spake by me, and His word was in my tongue.' David's affirmation is echoed over and over again by psalmist, historian, prophet, apostle and evangelist. Now the men who gave us the literature of the Old and New Testaments may, of course, have been wrong in their view that God had spoken to them—but they certainly believed it! To them inspiration was a living fact. They might not understand all they wrote, but they were quite sure that it came from above. Would they not have laughed at the idea that they were only arranging ancient and half-mythical material in a new form, or thrusting on posterity a private and highly tendentious account of certain historical incidents? No; something happened inside their soul—a burst of 'God-breathed' illumination—the result of which was Holy Scripture. Our Lord himself accepted that. He spoke with profound reverence of the scriptures as being the Word of God. He took them as completely authoritative for his own life and conduct, and settled many a religious quandary with the pronouncement 'It is written. . . .'

Of course no matter what view we take of the Bible, it will leave us with unsolved problems. These are necessarily bound up with such a revelation. Much harm has been done by the idea that the scriptures ought to be completely comprehensible to the human intellect. Men forget that 'His thoughts are higher than our thoughts.' It has been said that 'If the reality of God were small enough to be grasped, it would not be great enough to be adored.' No one in his senses would want to take every word of the Bible literally. There are some disputed passages where scholarship must be allowed to guide us in the exact reading of the text. But the Bible as a whole is what God meant it to be. These are the books He foreordained should be written. He made the men who acted as His scribes. He knew the limitations of their mind and heart. He gave them freedom to compose according to the laws of their nature. He arranged that they should address the world of their time in the language and concepts of their own day. Yet it was all His from first to last. It bears the stamp of His authority. It uttered the message He wanted to give. It was written not for that age alone but for all succeeding ages. The very form of it was to last for ever.

We need then to approach the Bible as we approach no other book. It is not ours to cut and carve according to our learned ingenuity. One's mind shrinks with a sense of horror from the complacent and quite unprovable assumptions that mar so many commentaries. Who are we to impose upon the Sacred Volume our own ideas of what it ought to teach? Surely our business is to receive the Bible message like Paul's friends at Salonika 'not as the word of men, but as it is in truth the word of God.' That means giving up the attempt to hammer it into an intellectually acceptable shape. There will be enigmas in it till the end of time. Says John Newton, writing to a friend, 'I beg you to be on your guard against a reasoning spirit. Search the scriptures . . . and be not discouraged because you may not be clearly able to answer or reconcile every difficulty that may occur. . . . Our hearts are very dark and narrow, and the very root of all apostacy is a proud disposition to question . . . divine appointments. But the child-like simplicity of faith is to follow God without reasoning; taking it for granted that a thing must be right if He directs it, and charging all seeming inconsistencies to the account of our own ignorance.' Profoundly wise!

A second thing the preacher will have to do is To Avoid Making An Idol of Human Reason. Of course we are to love the Lord with all our mind. There are very good grounds why the Church should insist on an educated Ministry. God is Truth. And it therefore behoves us to enquire into the reality of things. We should be able to speak out of an instructed understanding and to give a reason for the faith that is in us. A lad who dawdles through his student years is making a mistake which cannot afterward be remedied. Admittedly there have been some very effective preachers who were ignorant of academic disciplines. God can take a man from the work-bench or the counting-house and touch his lips with the altar fire. But the Church would not be justified in organising her pedagogy on the exceptional case. Most of us are average. If we are to minister with growing usefulness throughout our whole life we require to undergo training. A college background provides a man with the intellectual resources which he will need long after his first few sermons have vanished into limbo. Therefore glorious is the time when we ' sit among the doctors, hearing and asking them questions.' No better gift can any student take away from a theological hall than the memory of some devout and erudite teacher who first introduced him to the splendours of sacred scholarship. It does us all the good in the world to exercise our brain. So we should read, read, read, debate and argue, track down the literature, widen our horizons, and lay up stores of knowledge for the days to come.

And yet while that counsel is given from the heart, it needs to be accompanied by a warning. Every fine thing in this world has its dangers—even the golden period we spend in college. Unless we keep in view that our business is to become heralds of God we may end up as mere worshippers of learning. There is a type of mind fostered by study which comes perilously close to believing that only what can be rationally demonstrated is true and therefore worthy of our adherence. That is to say, discipleship is founded on knowledge rather than on faith. What is this but the ancient Gnostic heresy? Pride takes many forms. In every age the battle to extirpate it from the Church has to be fought again. We must learn to pursue the Truth, and yet not to rely on our own cleverness.

It is possible for a man to find when he goes out to his life-work that he has acquired an academic point of view which stultifies his ministry. This does not happen to all. It has certainly happened to some. Unknown to himself the individual concerned has allowed the bias of certain schools of thought to influence him unduly, not realising that their doctrine is disruptive of the Faith. But contact with his lay environment soon makes this clear. Asked to deal with human need, he searches in vain for any answer to it in terms of his theology. A dark day may even arrive when he begins to wonder why his spirit within him has turned to ashes. His case is put in the stabbing sentence, 'How dreadful to have a pulpit; but no message!' He has no message. NO MESSAGE. Of course he still has an experience; but he cannot communicate it now in these inadequate symbols.

So if any man suspects that he has built up too intellectualist an attitude during his student years, he is well advised to get rid of it before he enters his first charge. Not rid of his mind. Not rid of his learning. But rid of the critical approach, the habit of doubt, the subservience to great names, the near-contempt for old-fashioned believers. What he needs now is certainty. How can a man preach if he is not *sure* that the Bible is the Word of God?—if every text can be questioned?—if the statements are coloured by propaganda?—if Jesus was not virgin-born?—if He did not really work miracles?—if He did not die to pay the ransom-price?—if He was not raised up from the grave with the same body in which He suffered, though wonderfully changed?—if He was mistaken in His belief that He would come again at the end of the age in power and great glory? The trouble with such a view of the Gospel facts is that it won't preach. No man can put his heart into it. Only his head. There is all the difference in the world between a sermon on the Atonement which makes every pardoned sinner magnify God for the shed blood of Jesus Christ, and a sermon which explains that there never actually was any Atonement but that what is so described was only an incident containing certain mysterious 'religious values.' That sort of thing is useless in the pastoral ministry.

So even while we thank God for religious scholarship and freely acknowledge the debt we owe to it, let us remember that the secrets of the Kingdom are sometimes hid from the wise and prudent and revealed unto babes, and that our Lord rejoices to have it so. If our object as preachers were to impart 'man's wisdom' we should have to arm ourselves with an abundance of facts and reasoning power. But for the imparting of 'God's wisdom' what is required above all else is not knowledge but faith—a surrendered heart, a personality filled with grace. Somehow we have to love God with all our mind and yet realise the limitations of that particular instrument as a vehicle of divine knowledge. Paul was careful to point out to his friends at Corinth that his preaching ' was not with enticing words of man's wisdom but in demonstration of the Spirit and of power.' God's Word contains an element of mystery. It is not reducible to the rationalities of men. So we must beware of ' great swelling words of vanity ' and of ' the oppositions of science, falsely so-called.' Learning alone—mere learning, unqualified by common-sense and unillumined by divine insight—is apt to be self-deceived.

In his memoirs ('Along The Road To Frome ') Christopher Hollis tells how at Oxford in the early 1920's when the New Psychology was being talked of everywhere, he and some student friends staged a ' rag ' to de-bunk its excessive pretensions. Together they made up a lecture full of technical terms, but so constructed as to be absolutely meaningless. One of the party who spoke fluent German dressed himself to look like a mythical professor from the Continent. Advertised as Dr. Emil Busch of Vienna, he delivered this high-sounding nonsense to a crowded and distinguished audience in the Town Hall. ' The lecture,' says Hollis, ' went off without a hitch or a suspicion. It was applauded, and votes of thanks were moved. A female don, emerging from the Hall, was heard to confess that she had never previously been able to understand what the New Psychology was all about, but now, at last, Dr Busch had made it all clear. . . .'

Yes; it takes a good deal of grace to extract the best from our student years and yet not to lose the sharp native reactions of our religious consciousness. Unless we are on our guard against this danger we shall tend increasingly to trust in human logic. Our heroes become scholars rather than saints. We are more impressed by the brilliant man who can answer all our questions than by the merely devout man who stumbles over his replies. We may even be persuaded to swallow almost any statement, however unlikely or absurd, as long as it is vouched for by 'the experts.' But what if they are the victims of their own cleverness? There are fashions in theology just as in clothes, and quite a few of them are unrelated to divine truth and human need. When one ponders the work of some so-called 'revolutionary Christian thinkers' today, one feels moved to suggest that they must be self-deluded. Otherwise they would spare us volume after volume of tangled verbiage which (as far as we can grasp its meaning) often appears to be a denial of the 'things most surely believed among us.' Indeed if we want to hear the accents of the historic Christian faith in our time we may have to worship with some group of simple souls whose message, though it seems crude, is in many cases unmistakably what the New Testament teaches—salvation by the blood of Jesus.

A third essential condition for uttering the Gospel message is that *The Preacher Should Live In The Bible World*. He must surrender himself to the environment of holy scripture. There is a total difference between respecting the Bible as a religious classic and living by the Bible as one's daily and all-sufficient guide. 'I beseech you,' said Hew Binning, 'take the scriptures for the Rule of your walking, or else you will wander; the Scripture is *Regula Regulans*, a ruling Rule. If you be not acquainted with it, you must follow the opinions or examples of other men, and what if they lead you to destruction?' Granted that there is room for the use of sanctified common-sense in matters not dealt with by the Bible. But the number of such things—things that have to be ascertained and judged without the help of scripture—is far less than people think. Indeed this is perhaps the most startling discovery which many people make when their eyes are opened to behold the truth of God in His own Word. No longer is the Bible something outside their life to which they refer merely for corroboration of views which they have arrived at independently. *It* speaks first. One of General Gordon's biographers writes, 'Hitherto he had thought of the Bible as a sacred historical book. . . . Now it came to him that the Scriptures are still "alive," *oratio recta*, not *oratio obliqua*.' Thousands have had the very same experience. With a shock of delight they learned that they could now go to the Word of God for guidance on almost every problem with which they were confronted.

So the preacher instead of making up his mind by the light of ordinary intelligence and then looking for a Bible verse, or verses, to substantiate his findings goes straight to the fountain-head. If he wants to know what he should believe about anything—marriage, for example—before he even thinks of turning to a reference volume or consulting the latest pronouncement of an Assembly committee, he lifts his Bible; and with the help of a concordance, balancing scripture against scripture, soon sees for himself what God has been pleased to reveal to us on that question. It is the same with every other. More often than we allow, the answer even to controversial issues is quite simple, once we let God speak to us. But to hear it we must read the Bible, listen to the Bible, ponder the Bible, discuss the Bible, ransack the Bible, go to bed with the Bible, wake up in the morning with the Bible still at hand. We must know it; and we must obey it. That is the royal road to pulpit efficiency. D. L. Moody began (as many of us do) by taking his sermon-subjects from the life around him. But one day Henry Moorehouse came to his church in Chicago, and after listening for a while said, ' If you will stop preaching your own words and preach God's Word, you will make yourself a great power for good.' His suggestion fell on a heart ready to receive it, and Moody began to ' preach the Word in season, out of season ' with results which are known in their fulness only to the recording angel.

What a transformation is wrought when a man enters the Bible world! It is as if he had been lifted out of a flat featureless existence into a higher dimension. This new sphere has depth, perspective, undertones and overtones. We can look back now at what is called ' the real world ' and suddenly see it for the unsatisfying and perishing thing it is. Indeed we wonder that we ever found it tolerable before. And not only have our surroundings been changed, but so has the whole character of life. ' We walk,' as Alistair MacLean says, ' in Happy Safety.' Difficulties vanish. Prayer is answered. Means are provided. Healing restores us. We leave our concerns in God's hands, sure that they will be attended to. We expect guidance in every personal problem, down to the smallest detail. The Book itself ' comes alive ' as moment-by-moment direction from the Almighty. Hence the fondness of some devout souls for scripture calendars, wall texts, promise-boxes and the like. Of course all this may be regrettable in the view of those who advocate a critically-grounded faith; and yet it is quite startling how often such simple things are blessed. It would almost seem as if God enjoyed our making the childlike approach. When we walk by the Word, we live on the edge of miracle. Nothing astonishes us any more because we have left the ordinary bounds of possibility far behind. So we no longer doubt the extraordinary coincidences which mark out a believer's way. In these, as in much else that happens to us, we detect ' the meer finger of God.'

Having accepted the scriptures as the Word of God, having put away the delusions of the natural reason, and having begun to live in the Bible world, *a man soon discovers that his message shows a characteristic amplitude.* It is bigger than the thing one hears in many pulpits. It contains subjects which the bulk of men seldom deal with —as, for example, promises made to believers, the reality of guidance, heaven's offer to heal, the place of fasting, the ministry of angels, the Devil and his works, the end of the age, the second coming of our Lord, the future blessedness of the redeemed and the future punishment of the wicked. It is not that these things were absent from the scriptures. On the contrary, they stand in the forefront. But men seem to be blind. Dominated by theological prejudice they simply leave out, by an unconscious censorship, what they do not rationalistically approve. Yet the moment any of us sit down with the Bible, willing to learn, we discover that these things must be accorded a place with the very marrow of our message. It is just as important to canvass them as it is to declare ' the word of the Cross.' They belong to the same transcendental environment. They witness to the sovereignty of God, the lordship of Jesus Christ, and the present action of the Holy Spirit.

Furthermore, once he is at home in the Bible world, *the view a man takes of his mission becomes equally distinctive and unusual*. Formerly, though he called himself ' preacher ' he really thought of himself as primarily a teacher. He was in the pulpit to educate church-goers in things divine; and as there was no hurry at all, he could afford to do that in a systematic and leisurely way. He wanted to help people in their struggles, showing them the same quiet courtesy that Jesus showed on the Galilean hillside. But now, as he re-reads the Gospels, he begins to perceive that underneath that tranquil exterior our Lord was always thrusting forward with every nerve astrain toward a goal. There were only twelve hours in the day, and he had much to do before he could cry ' It is finished!' Something of that same intensity grips the Bible preacher. His time-scale is shortened. He surveys life's landscape not by the philosophic light of reason but by apocalyptic flashes that presage a coming act of God. His task, as he now understands it, is in great measure that of a lifeguard whose first business is to rescue men and women from a fearful doom. Does not the whole New Testament bear witness that apart from God they are lost for ever?

This dreadful certainty rings in his ears like an alarm-bell. The modern world does not of course believe it. And perhaps the modern Church does not quite believe it either. She has, at least in thought, cut down the famous Johannine verse to read, 'God so loved the world that He gave His only-begotten Son that whosoever believeth in Him should have everlasting life.' There is no such scripture. What the Bible says is 'that whosoever believeth in Him *should not perish* but have everlasting life.' Without Christ men are perishing. That was why God sent His Son. That was why there was a Cross on Calvary. That is why we must be re-born from above. To take away 'should not perish' is to cancel out the reason for redemption. John III, 16, then becomes merely an announcement of what God is. It loses all force as a declaration of what God has done. The truth is that He initiated this work because ours is a fallen order which needs to be reconciled to the One Who created it. So the Bible-believing preacher is naturally filled with the same motive. He walks through the common ways of life with this divine urgency burning in his breast—'should not perish,' 'should not perish,' 'should not perish.' That is what the whole thing is *for*. The Church. His Pulpit. Next week's sermon. One more chance to cry aloud. It is all 'that they should not perish but have everlasting life.'

The evolutionist idea that we grow upward from lowly beginnings to a higher and yet higher state of moral excellence is contradicted by fact. It is also repudiated by the Bible. Almost on its opening page we learn of man's fall through disobedience, and of the corruption that ensued. Some of its last pages outline God's judgment on a wicked earth when this planet will be consumed in flaming fire. So the testimony of God's Word is that men are 'lost' because of sin, and therefore doomed not only in a physical sense but spiritually also. Allowance will of course be made for those of every nation who have walked faithfully according to the light they have received. But generally speaking what the Levites in the Book of Nehemiah said of the Jewish people is still true of multitudes beside, 'They rebelled against Thee, and cast Thy law behind their backs, and slew Thy prophets which testified against them . . . and . . . wrought great provocations.'

The preacher's business is to arouse these people and to rescue them from the doom which certainly awaits. He must not be turned aside from his purpose by their outward seeming. Sin is a disease of the interior life. It need not necessarily have any immediate effect upon the carriage men show to the world. Yet for some strange reason we tend to associate it with a sordid and brutalised appearance. Even yet the typical 'sinner' is for most folk the ill-clad drunken wreck so often portrayed by Victorian evangelists. His 'lostness' was physically obvious. It could hardly fail to be noted. But today this long-standing link which sin used to have with disease and destitution has passed away. Many quite shocking sinners are handsome and beautifully dressed. As we gaze at these attractive folk it is hard to believe that Paul's description of them is still true—cheats, thieves, liars, bullies, traitors, scoundrels, perverts, adulterers, perhaps even murderers. Are they really like that? Yes, they are. There has been no mistake. If they are allowed to remain in their present condition they will end in torment at the last. People who live without God, or against God, are already perishing.

How small is the realisation of these things at the present hour!—even in the pulpit. After Joshuah had gathered the congregation of Israel we are told that he read in their hearing 'all the words of the law, the blessing *and the curse. . . .*' Nobody reads the curse today; only the blessing. The mood of our time is as calm and easy as it was before the Deluge. There is little consciousness of sin, still less that God should have been at such desperate measure to cope with it. From an examination of the general outlook one might be pardoned for thinking that this whole business had been grossly exaggerated. How can all these nice, clean, well-dressed people be 'lost'? Have we not a higher standard of living than ever before? What of television, social security, miracle drugs, and the universal family car? But our great Authority once asked, 'What shall it profit a man if he shall gain the whole world and lose his own soul?' For it is the soul that is of lasting importance; not all this trash of material comforts. They have no value for eternity. The very man who owns them now may be already damned. So God has a terrible problem to face. Most of us don't even believe in its existence. But He does; and He could conceive no answer short of Calvary.

Speaking to His Father, Jesus said, 'Those that Thou gavest me I have kept, and none of them is lost but the son of perdition, that the scripture might be fulfilled.' None of them is lost. What an achievement! Can we by divine help in some small measure make it ours? At anyrate we must seize upon any available means toward this end. Our business is to publish the good news of salvation. There is no room and no time in our pulpit for anything less than the Gospel. We must have a message. Every man will find it for himself in the broad reaches of scripture. It may come from the Old Testament or the New. But it will proclaim the whole counsel of God and apply it to the hearer with unmistakable fidelity. No one must ever be allowed to go away from Public Worship with the feeling that it was all irrelevant, or that we didn't seem to care. They must be told how God loves them, how He has always loved them, and how He loves them still with a passion undiminished. We have the answer to the soul-wants of the human race. When they look toward the pulpit they should see a door swing back upon its hinges and open out on the eternal world. The unseen should become plainly visible to the eye of faith. Its beauty, its holiness, its profound satisfactions should make men desire it. And they will, if we have done our work beforehand. Every preacher as he mounts the pulpit on a Sunday morning should be able to say with Jim Elliot the Auca martyr, 'Last night . . . great sweeping desires for the glory of God seized upon me. . . .' O that they might hear! O that they might believe!

But if they refuse the message, we must go on to warn them of the consequences. And perhaps this is the more necessary because it is so generally neglected in our time. Not that we would have any man become a 'hell-fire ranter.' And yet, as Jonathan Edwards truly says, 'If there really be a hell . . . why is it not proper for those who have the care of souls to take great pains to make men sensible of it?' We must not neglect our duty. There is too much at stake. Millions both inside and outside the Church are perishing because we have given them only half the Bible message—the kindness but not the severity of God. By all means let us preach the love of Christ in its unsearchable immensity; but let us also bear in mind that it was he himself, the Prince of Love, who spoke the gravest words that ever fell from human lips about the fate of the impenitent. We are soul-winners. When we know that a life lived in wilful neglect of God finishes in darkness and torment, we should be stirred to plead with our brother. The Texas Rangers have a wonderful motto, 'No man in the wrong can stand up against a fellow that's in the right—and keep coming.' We are in the right. Let *us* keep coming, Sunday after Sunday, with the only message that can ever save the souls of men.

III

OUR LISTENING CONGREGATION

THE preacher requires an audience. There must be those who wait on his word. Theoretically he is entitled to address any casual gathering, in a city square, on the village green, or by the sea-shore sands. But ours is no longer the wholly unevangelised world of the New Testament. A Christian Church has been pouring its blessings on this island for thirteen or fourteen hundred years. Therefore in practice the would-be herald's freedom is limited. He has, of course, the unrestricted right to preach in places where the Gospel has never been heard of—which would mean some heathen territory overseas. But we are thinking chiefly of the home field; and that raises a very different issue. It *is* a question whether any man should begin preaching at his own sweet will in an area which already has an abundance of Christian ordinances. The particular representatives of the Lord's household whom he finds there may not be uttering exactly what he would; but the variation is probably so small as to make no difference to the eternal standing of believers. So before he opens his mouth, he ought to ask himself whether he is justified in doing so.

There has always been both an itinerant and a settled ministry. God does raise up once in a while some notable ambassador who cannot easily be fitted into the mould of any existing denomination. Acknowledging that, we should nevertheless be chary of the self-appointed preacher. While break-away tactics have sometimes been forced on zealous souls by the coldness or unconcern of the official Church, the reason for spurning authority is not always so altruistic. Indeed private evangelistic effort in the modern world may be due to nothing more exalted than a determination to be one's own master. No one person should be sole judge in his own case. It is not for him to say what the Church needs or how he ought to serve it. The true preacher will normally await a commission from his brethren as well as from the Lord.

As a general rule he will also have a church, a designated building in which he conducts the Services. The New Testament ' house-church ' was an emergency measure only. It bridged the gap between leaving the synagogue and fashioning a new temple for Christian worship. It was never intended to become permanent except in the localised sense that every believing home will set up a family altar. Men have, of course, preached, as Jesus Himself did, under the open sky; and sometimes to vast multitudes. One thinks of Savonarola; or of Wesley and Whitefield; or of Alexander Peden in the moss-hags of Ayrshire, and Richard Cameron on a haugh near New Monkland, and John Welsh opening the scriptures to the saints by the waterside of Tweed. But these were exceptional instances due to evangelical necessity or the unsettled character of the times. Ordinarily a preacher has a church. And what is more he has a pulpit. Some of us can never stand there without being deeply moved.

We run our fingers reverently along the worn velvet of the Bible cushion and feel encircling us the strength of the panelled wood. Or at least we do so in churches which have not exchanged that noble and significant piece of furniture for a tiny brass lectern. There are pulpits so majestic that they almost make a man a preacher; and there are others so unsuited to their Gospel business that they snuff him out.

A minister of the Establishment enjoys one advantage over some of his brethren. While he willingly admits that they—if they hold a different theological position—are fully entitled to publish it abroad, he at anyrate does not have to defend or justify the right to preach on what we may term 'his own ground.' The nation has willed that Christian ordinances should be made officially available there; and he is the individual who has been appointed by the Church to provide them. His 'cure of souls' is to a large extent circumscribed by geographic boundaries. He therefore preaches in one place and to one particular group of people, often over a long period of time. This gives his ministry a quite distinctive 'family' character. There are of course some charges, especially in the centre of great cities, where a relatively large proportion of those at Public Worship consists of visitors and strangers. If the site itself is historic, or if it has been made famous by some illustrious name, crowds may stream in at the church door all the year round. Such 'metropolitan tabernacles' can be very stimulating, and they provide an unusual opportunity for a preacher with special gifts. But they are relatively few. The great majority of ordained men live and labour within their own parish, confronting the same people Sunday after Sunday.

Now one of the important things about a ' family ' is that though recognisable as a common social unit, it is also different from every other of its kind. No two families are the same. Nor are any two congregations. This is a fact of which ecclesiastical administrators seem, on the whole, to be insufficiently aware. Not that they can be blamed for it. Their job is to see the general beyond the particulars. But, alas, the particulars are often so very particular that there is almost no general left with which to deal! Each congregation is unique. It may belong to the suburbs or the town; to the farm-lands or the sea; it may be clever or stupid, generous or mean, friendly or aloof, vulgar or well-bred, spiritually-minded or worldly to the point of open disgrace. It is therefore not possible to lay down laws which will apply neatly and effectively to all congregations. Things can be done in one the very hint of which would be quite unrealistic in another only fifty yards away. For there is no such thing as ' a congregation '; there is only ' this congregation ' or ' that congregation '; and each has to be known from the inside before it can be understood.

The fact that a preacher is supplied with a body of trysted hearers lays him under a three-fold obligation. First, *COMMITMENT TO HIS PARISH*. When he was inducted to this charge he gave himself utterly to its people. He is theirs and they are his. He folds them to his heart. He accepts their background and traditions. Therefore he identifies himself completely with their way of life. This shows in various small habit-changes. For example, he may give up the (to him) familiar newspaper which none of his flock ever read, and take the one which mirrors their environment. Or he may stop making long journeys 'home' to obtain certain professional services and start using those which are available at his own door. For he wants to become part of the community in which he dwells. However isolated his charge, he refuses to think of himself as an exile from some brighter sphere. *This* is his sphere. This is the very centre of things. Some have looked on the whole world as their parish; he prefers to treat the parish as his world. If that be a humbler vocation, it is often more effective and rewarding for the average servant of God.

The parish church is of course the focus of the family's life. Once a week comes the hour for which the preacher has longed when they wend their way to the House of God. How it melts his heart to look down on them!—the same folk in the same pews. These are the Lord's anointed gathered 'all with one accord in one place' for the holiest of human exercises. 'Let Us Worship God!' he says; and they lift the opening psalm to the sweet simplicity of 'French,' or the meditative rise and fall of 'Dunfermline,' or the morning brightness of 'London New'—or, on great days, the pealing chords of the 'Old Hundredth.' He misses the folk who are not there; especially the look of certain corners from which some cherished saint has been translated to glory within the Sabbath octave. How true it is that 'No man preaches to a congregation; he preaches to a procession'!

> Part of His host hath crossed the flood,
> And part is crossing now.

Yet, change as they will, they are nevertheless his own. Here he beholds the little ones just sacred at the font; there the couples he has married; yonder the aged, now so lonely, whom he can perhaps remember as they once were in their thronging years. With every twelvemonth that goes by this entire household sits more closely to his bosom. He understands now that word which an ex-Moderator gave him in his early days, 'My dear lad, at the beginning you will have your congregation—*and* your friends. But after a while you will find that your congregation *are* your friends.'

That raises the question of tenure. How long is he to stay with them? For it is obvious that no man can develop a pastoral heart if he is never long enough with any one congregation to know it through and through. The Gaelic noun for 'Induction' is the same as that for 'Marriage.' So in Presbyterian Scotland a man is always settled in a charge for the duration of his natural life. Circumstances may of course arise in which he is invited to transfer his ministry elsewhere; and he may then (after a reasonable length of service) be guided to do so. But even in that case those who ask for his removal must satisfy the presbytery that this divorce is likely to have results more advantageous to the Church at large than the existing marriage. Modern presbyteries are inclined to take this duty of judgment far too lightly. Hence a misguided incumbent may start a whole series of so-called ' significant and challenging experiments,' the upkeep of which would soon crush any man of normal vigour, and then after three or four hectic years dash off to pastures new. Even in agriculture it is a serious offence to initiate a cycle of over-production which leaves the land exhausted for the next tenant. Is there any reason why a cleric who does that with his parish should not be judged guilty of exploiting the Lord's vineyard? A man should consider very carefully whether he has the right to begin what he is not prepared to finish.

So we must stay with our people until the Holy Spirit bears witness with our spirit that our work in that place is done. God is a God of reason. He does not plant a man in one corner of the field only to uproot him and send him to another before harvest. The length of our ministry in a particular parish may not be under our control, because ' Calls ' tends to cease after a certain age; but the brevity usually is. During the first half of life at anyrate, the decision *when to leave* is in our own hands. We can give a negative answer to those who would entice us away before our job is finished. Vacancies are costly and upsetting things. They nearly always do harm. There is a danger, admittedly, in an over-long pastorate; but it is seldom anything like as great as that involved in a series of short-term ministries. A garden needs time to grow. A flock needs time to mature.

Our second duty is *COMPREHENSION OF THE PARISH*. We must know our people and the environment in which they earn their livelihood. There is one exception to that law. It does not hold of the special evangelist. As his sole business is to press for an immediate decision, it is almost an advantage that he should be a stranger. His appeal comes home with added force just because it is unqualified by any general considerations. But for parish preaching—preaching which relates the grace of God to our many-sided mundane life—an understanding of the folk in the pew is essential. We must be familiar with them in all the rich variety of their nature; their lovableness, their cares, their blind spots, their instinctive decency, their quiet heroisms, their secret longings after sainthood. We must be able to bring them the kind of message that will always touch the nerve. They must listen to 'their own man' (ungifted though he be) as they will listen to nobody else on earth. This requires that we should know a good number of them personally, indeed intimately. Rutherford, condemned to silence in a Northern jail, wrote to his flock at Anwoth, 'My soul longeth exceedingly to hear whether there be any work of Christ in the parish. . . . I think of my people in my sleep.' Happy is the man who can echo these words!

This degree of acquaintance was achieved by our forefathers through systematic visitation. They went round the parish house by house. And there is no doubt that that method worked very well in days when each town or village was a self-contained unit. It can still be used in certain areas with good results. But where the congregation is very large, widely scattered, or much affected by those technological and social changes which have altered the whole character of family life, it has been robbed of a great deal of its value. One of the most conscientiously house-going ministers in the West of Scotland who succumbed in his early fifties, wrote on his death-bed, ' If I had my ministry to do over again, I would pastor a great deal less and be a student of the Word all the more.' It is a mistake to let popular notions of how we *should* behave dominate our thinking. By all means let a man keep regular contact with every home in his parish, if he can do so without injuring his pulpit work. Certainly we should try to pay at least one domestic call on each new member who joins the congregation. But in big city charges, rather than attempt repeated visits of that kind, it may be found more advisable to lay a new and stronger emphasis on the friendly relationships established in the course of each day's round with those who inevitably cross our path. Sick visits, private interviews, congregational activities, baptisms, weddings, funerals, and suchlike engagements then become the chief means of learning about our flock. And these, arising as they do out of the traffic of life itself, have the advantage of making up in sheer natural intimacy for much of what we lose by want of card index thoroughness.

It is not necessary to follow any one particular method in caring for those under our leadership; but it is necessary to know them—our purpose being, of course, that they may hear the Word of God more effectively. Sermons have little value in themselves; their value lies in what they achieve. So if we are to reach a man's heart we must 'speak to his condition.' An evangelistic address can be composed anytime, anywhere, by a man who is not even attached to a local church. He makes his plea for decision with almost equal intelligibility in Glasgow or Galveston, Jersey or Johannesburg. But a sermon is quite different. It grows out of a living relationship between the preacher and his audience. They generate it as much as he—not the Word (which is God's Word) but the form in which it is cast and the manner in which the whole thing is presented. All that is their doing. So it is full of personal vibrations, subtle allusions, overtones and undertones which only those immersed in the pastoral situation can fully grasp. Much of it is therefore likely to be lost on the casual hearer. It is 'family talk.'

Preaching of this sort is seldom just the utterance of general truth. Nearly always it is a particular truth evoked by, adapted to, and intended for one people. Hence if a man be translated from a parish to other non-parochial work his friends often notice a distinct waning of his former instancy in the pulpit. The reason is that he dwells now in a world which does not beget sermons. Of course he may still at an occasional week-end deliver an excellent homily and be heard with acceptance. But the chances are that the mysterious 'something' which once enabled him to drive past the intellect into the life-changing region of the soul will have largely vanished. He has developed other aptitudes. God is generous with His gifts; but economical also. Those which we do not habitually use He takes away. It has been observed that ' when the famous David Dickson became a professor of Divinity he fell off in sweetness and force. " No wonder," he said, " for I have lost my books " —meaning by that his people.' Sermons are not things we *make,* as we might make a model ship. All the best sermons ' happen.' They are the result of that state of mind induced by pastoral intercourse with our flock. The moment we stop thinking about them, praying for them, moving among them, talking to them, working, rejoicing and sorrowing with them, we cease to be able to act in any full sense as ' heralds of God.' Our life is bound up with theirs. Preaching is merely the audible evidence of that relationship. If a man dislikes his hearers, or if he is busy trying to get away from them, he need not expect one single glory-hour in the pulpit.

Our third duty is *CONCENTRATION ON THE PARISH*. There are a few areas so thinly populated that unless a man feels called to advance theological learning or (like the enclosed religious) to engage in a special ministry of prayer, he would certainly have time on his hands. But not many of us are called to face that issue. The average parish is a whole-time job. So it is a mistake to think, as Chalmers did in his Kilmany days, that the fag-end of our time is enough for our sacred duties. If we are doing the work properly it will demand all that we can bring. Therefore to use up any large part of our life for interests and causes that lie outside the sphere of the holy ministry is to be false to our ordination vow. 'No man can serve two masters.' It is not for us to tell our Lord that we have discovered ways of getting round his statement of the impossible. Doubtless men are variously gifted. Some can do in a day what would cost others a week. And not all who bide within their own borders are free from laziness. But when that is granted, it still remains true that a parish will always suffer if its shepherd tries to live a divided life.

The great bulk of us are fully conscious of this, and do not even attempt it. But there is a lesser fault which may in the end have almost equally grave results. One of the commonest temptations of the ministry is to take our eye off the main thing. When the first few years of novelty are over, when some of his early dreams have failed to materialise, and when it becomes increasingly plain that even the best of those under his charge can 'resist the Spirit,' a man may begin to let his gaze wander. Feeling the need of relaxation from purely ministerial work, he embraces (let us say) some hobby which takes him into the garden, and later to various flower shows around the countryside. Or he discovers an unsuspected aptitude for the lecture platform which is more esteemed in distant towns that it is at his own door. Or he is attracted to committee work, with its frequent journeyings and its sense of involvement in great matters. Now, of course, we must all have some stimulus in life. And there are certain social and presbyterial obligations lying outside our immediate task to which we should devote part of our energies. Yet not to the extent of turning our leisure employment into our chief business. Only the individual himself can tell whether this is what has actually happened; and even to decide that may require an unusually honest act of self-judgment. But if it has, he ceases to be minister of the parish. The people may still get service, worthy and adequate as far as it goes; but they no longer get *him*. The deepest affection of his heart is bestowed elsewhere. All he has left to offer his own folk is the professional residue.

We shall never preach as Christ's ambassadors were meant to preach, with our whole soul crying out in every word, unless we love the men and women before us. And we cannot love them until we have accepted the fact that our destiny is there, in that particular spot. They were chosen as our flock from the very beginning. Therefore we are to see our parish in the light of eternity. And there is all the more need for this because it may be of such a sort as is calculated to depress. Indeed, if the truth were told there are few parishes that do not have some characteristic annoyance, stumbling-block, or limitation. The result is that even the most faithful of men may occasionally reach a point at which he feels he can endure it no longer. That humble saint, Thomas Boston—bearing so brave a testimony through fits of the gravel and numerous pastoral discouragements—once complained that he was 'staked in Ettrick.' Others have shared his feeling. And of course we have to admit the possibility that they *might* be the better of a change. But if our chief desire is simply to serve those for whose everlasting welfare God has made us accountable, then the likelihood is that once we have recovered from our temporary wanderlust, we shall still find all the conditions of a blessed ministry where we are. Nobody can stop us from being finally and gloriously effective if we concentrate on our own parish.

That brings us now to the great end for which the parish itself exists—the proclamation of the Word of God. Nothing more significant ever happens there than the utterance of the Gospel message on the Lord's Day. All else leads up to this. The minister's commitment to, comprehension of, and concentration on his ' cure of souls ' are the necessary preliminaries to his leading of Public Worship. And the sermon is the climax of that worship. Repeated attempts have been made to lay the emphasis elsewhere. But all to no purpose. The Scot knows by instinct what his ' subordinate standards ' already teach, namely, that the Word comes before the Sacraments. So he is obstinately sermon-minded; and just as obstinately opposed to any ' High ' church ceremonial. He can on great occasions bring himself to make a few responses. But he never does it with any inward comfort. It is alien to his nature. Perhaps, like C. S. Lewis, he has ' a boorish inaptitude for the collective.' But the fact that some sensitive spirits are a little ashamed of this does not change the condition one iota. So while we thank God for the liturgical revival of the late nineteenth century which has helped to correct our slipshod ways, yet any idea that the bulk of Scotsmen will ever find in liturgy alone, however chaste, the answer to the deepest need of their spirit, is purely chimerical. Sermons are our meat and drink. We look for them every week-end as a spiritual necessity.

Hence on the morning of the Lord's Day the preacher comes forth clothed with his message. This is the supreme hour—the thing for which he was born, the task to which he is called, the holy action that crowns his very existence. He approaches it with a sense of awe. And yet, portentous as the work is, it lays no burden on his spirit. Though quivering inwardly, he feels elated. In such employment he can afford to forget himself. Therefore there is a boldness about his presentation. He asks no man's leave. The pulpit girds him round with magisterial influence. For that in very truth is what a pulpit is—no mere device to make speech audible in large buildings, but a terrestrial counterpart of the heavenly throne. Before him sit the waiting people. He is conscious of their silent invitation. 'Now are we all here present before God, to hear all things that are commanded thee. . . .' Because he has wrought over the entire Service in detail, coughs will be few. Here is no shambling lackadaisical crowd, but a trained body of listeners. They know that their pastor is prepared. Always. And they are ready too. The atmosphere is expectant. When he comes forward to the Book and says 'Let Us Worship God' they are launched once more through praise and prayer on that solemn exercise which will lead them upward in its supreme moment to the very feet of their Maker.

Every preacher has a sermon; but his preaching is a much bigger thing than the sermon—which is why so few books of sermons give more than a faint and far-away echo of what actually happened. *That* can never go into any volume. It is an experience incommunicable. Nobody can share it except those who were there, locked into the church with the preacher. It cannot be known by reading an account of it afterward. It is a thing-in-itself, a once-for-all. The sermon was only the material the preacher used to bring about this result, just as an artist uses tubes and brushes to make a picture. Hence it is of no importance whether anybody remembers a word of it or not, because it was but a means to an end. It had (let us hope) some intellectual content; for, as the cynic says, 'Every sermon should contain at least one idea.' But preaching is not teaching and does not require to follow pedagogic patterns. The New Testament distinguishes between Kerygma and Didache; the former being the proclamation of the mighty works of God in Jesus Christ which the evangelist made to the outside world, the latter being the instruction about holiness which the minister of a congregation would give to his own people. The circumstances which produced that sharp distinction have largely disappeared. Most preaching now involves both Kerygma and Didache. But because they go together the teaching is seldom mere teaching. We must not suppose that once men and women are committed Christians they no longer need to hear the Gospel. On the contrary it is by listening again and again to the Good News that their faith is quickened and enriched.

The preacher then is not there to read an essay, or to give a lecture, or to expound a treatise. He is not there even to supply doses of comfort. He is there to deliver a message in the course of which men will hear God speak to their souls, and through that hearing be exalted to vision and union. The sermon is designed to create this ' mystical moment.' Something happens in true preaching; something supernatural. At a particular point in it (often about two thirds through) the heavens are opened and the church is filled with glory. We are conscious of the brush of wings and the brightness of fire. The Son of God has been lifted up, and he is now drawing all men unto him. This can happen to different folk at different stages in the drama; and each worshipper would describe it in his or her own language. But it should happen, in recognisable though varying degree, every Sunday. And people must know that it has happened. This is what validates worship. Something is *done*. A miracle is wrought. Our need is answered. The link between man and his Maker is re-established. When people attend that kind of church they come away with the remark, ' I never go there but I get something.'

Always the preacher addresses his flock with one specific end in view. ' We preach . . . that we may present every man perfect in Christ Jesus.' That is the purpose of sermons, irrespective of the means by which they are delivered. They were not agonised into existence in order that they might read well in some publisher's Christmas list several years afterward—though they may have a certain value there. Originally they were tools for a job. The man who delivered them hoped that with the assistance of divine grace they would be used for the re-shaping of human nature until it was changed into the image of the Lord. If they have had no such influence on anybody, they have failed; and we shall be called to account for it. After all, if the preacher had been in business—for example, as a cattle breeder or a building contractor—he would be expected to show some solid achievement for his work at the end of the day. Why should we think that because spiritual things are harder to assess than material ones, we are therefore excused? 'I want to come,' said St Paul to the Romans, 'so as to have some *results* among you.'

There are two mistakes into which we are apt to fall concerning results. The first is that because they are by their very nature often invisible, and known perfectly only to God, we need not worry our heads about them. But such an authority as Charles Haddon Spurgeon will have none of that. Analysing the attitude of these easy-going keepers of the vineyard, he says profoundly, 'Is it their belief that Paul plants and Apollos waters, and that God gives no increase? Vain are their talents . . . without the signs following. Prophets whose words are powerless, sowers whose seed all withers, fishers who take no fish, soldiers who give no wounds—are these God's men?

Surely it were better to be a mud-raker or a chimney-sweep, than to stand in the ministry as an utterly barren tree?' Conscience tells us that in the main he is right. We ought to have some evidence that the Spirit is at work. For to our shame be it said that we have sometimes been guilty of exercising a ministry which could no more produce a new Christian than a skeleton can bear a living child.

The second mistake is the very opposite of the first, namely, a brash confidence that there must always be visible results, and that we are fully qualified to estimate their worth. This leads some enthusiastic believers almost to force God's hand. They are quite sure that all His ways are entirely comprehensible by the redeemed intellect. They see the world as already divided into sheep and goats, saved and unsaved, and themselves as gifted with infallible judgment for discriminating between them. A young and evangelically-minded minister on his first trip to the United States spoke to a number of religious groups among the student fraternity. In almost every case a high percentage of the members belonged to some branch of the Church. But in the report which he sent back to England, the minister explained that he was leaving the University of A. and going to the University of B. because there was a considerable body of ' Christians ' there. In short, he seemed able to detect ' Christians ' from among the generality of God's people as easily as one picks out a man in uniform from the civilian crowd. It is not as simple as that.

The herald of God stands committed to a dual task. He is both evangelist and teacher. That is to say, he must strive for people's conversion, and yet he must aim also at their sanctification. In this respect our own Church today is very one-sided. Most of her pulpits lay an almost exclusive emphasis on the management of the Christian Life. Few speak of its origin. Yet we cannot ignore Christ's challenge to the unconverted without losing the tone and temper of a redeeming fellowship. We must pray for revival. Preachers should expect conversions. Then they will go out on the Sabbath with the knowledge that the power of the Holy Ghost may overshadow the people; the fire may fall from heaven; and some lost soul, having found the Saviour, may go to bed that night ' tired with the weight of glory.' Few things are so thrilling as to hear a man or woman suddenly of their own free will confess:

'Tis done! the great transaction's done!
I am my Lord's and He is mine.

What an ecstatic moment that is!—to kneel beside the new-born soul and see it pass through the gates into the Kingdom.

If a man has never had such an experience he has yet to make full proof of his ministry. But let him take comfort. ' The wonders that our fathers told ' are still being enacted at the present hour. Several years ago the Church built an ' extension ' charge in a new housing area which was full of families taken from poorish tenements, some indeed from the city slums. At the opening Act of Worship the minister said to a fellow-presbyter, ' This is a great job! All these folk are getting a fresh start. They want to do everything right this time. There's magic in the air!' Yes; there always is when we are suddenly given a new lease of life. And if the preacher knew how many of those who sit before him at the week-end crave inwardly for a fresh start, he would have less hesitation in 'making the appeal' and calling upon his hearers to close now with Jesus Christ. Any man who after a season of faithful work feels that the hour has come, and risks it, will usually be amazed at the response.

The truth is that many people *want* to be evangelised. Their whole being leaps up in joy to match the Gospel word. Of course they don't want the thing done crudely or offensively. But they are sick of their sins. They are frightened at the evil habits which they don't seem to have strength enough to conquer. And so when they come to church on Sunday, there is at the back of their mind a wistful hope that perhaps the man of God may be able by divine assistance to do for them what they cannot do for themselves, namely, to warm their whole nature, to melt their stubborn heart, and to lead them to that pitch of resolution where they will lay their life with utter abandonment at the feet of Jesus Christ. Not that they always intend to signify this in some external way, like walking out to the front or signing a card. The appeal may have involved no such obligation. Scotsmen are reticent in religious matters; and many of them are quite well able to pass through the 'saving change' without human witness or helper of any kind. But it stirs the flock to realise that when they gather for worship they meet at the edge of miracle. The Church is not just an institution for perpetuating a holy routine; it is a soul-saving agency.

Of course we must not exaggerate the possibilities of an ordinary parish. 'Times of refreshing' are unusual. The Church does not—and could not—luxuriate continually under pentecostal showers. Such unremitting emotionalism would ruin God's husbandry. Therefore we have dry days even in the finest congregation. The members themselves are very varied in spiritual attainment and cannot all be fitted into the one pattern. Immaturity believes that there are certain 'right people' who form the true church. Maturity teaches us that there is no perfect church, no ideal religious group, no homogeneous collection of saints. But it also enables us to perceive that wherever Christ is, there His work is going on. Thousands of quiet people entirely innocent of any flamboyant conversion experience are nevertheless true disciples of the Lord. They speak no special language. They are not even endowed with any marked religious gift. But they are church products through and through.

We have every right then to look for results; but we must also have faith to believe that they are there, even when we cannot see them. Take a trip to Loch Ard and gaze at the Government-owned forest. Go back a month afterward and study it once more. Nothing seems to have changed. Yet experts say that in the interval it has added two million feet of new timber, and grown in value by £22,000. The Church too is a living organism in which there is perpetual increase. But much of that may be so even, regular, and slow as to escape our faculty of discernment. ' God's word never returns unto Him void.' It changes people's thoughts and influences their conduct. It helps them with their problems and enables them to endure and overcome their trials. Indeed as the years pass by they often begin to walk in ways which at the start would have seemed for them quite out of character. Many a young man in his first charge has been humbled to find that folk whom he judged ' unspiritual ' were cultivating a life of secret devotion that put his own to shame. No; we have no cause to fear for the Church of the Living God. Even in the dullest deadest parish there are saints by whom it is glorified.

Hence it is very foolish to be always engaged in head-counting. The fact that on one notable day ' there were added to the church about three thousand souls ' was set down to inspire future generations. But much Holy Ghost work is beyond all earthly arithmetic. For full understanding there we shall have to wait until the books are opened. People are very mysterious. We cannot know the whole of any living personality. Always it has vices that balance its virtues and strange contradictions which are quite beyond us to resolve. So we must go forward in faith, rejoicing in any triumphs which God permits us to see, but not demanding them as a condition of our discipleship, nor losing heart when the results seem meagre. Perhaps what we most need is the grace of continuance. To ' keep at it, in season, out of season.' And above all, to be ready every Sabbath for the waiting congregation. That is our destiny; the hour in which our little life attains its true and full significance. So the pulpit becomes a numinous place; another Bethel that casts a hush over our spirit. 'To the end of my preaching life,' says a famous churchman, 'I could never enter a pulpit without the feeling that I was facing a crisis. . . . Often in later years, as the verger closed the door behind me . . . I would utter that prayer which is the summary of all prayers, "In tuas manus, Domine, meam animam commisi."' There could be no more fitting utterance for a spokesman of the Eternal.

IV

SOME HELPFUL TECHNIQUES

WHEN Kathleen Ferrier, the world-famous contralto, was a child about three years of age, she began to finger the piano, dancing round it and striking a few notes here and there. One day, in an effort to show her prowess to a cousin who had just arrived, she sat down at the keyboard and picked out a halting little tune. ' But ' (says her biographer) ' the next moment she burst into a passion of tears. " What's the matter, love?" asked her cousin. " I want to play," sobbed Kathleen, " I want to play—and I can't play properly!" ' The music inside the child was crying for expression, but she was not yet trained to bring it forth. Isn't that like the difficulty of a young preacher? He has a message pent up in his heart; but he soon learns that he cannot put it into words with anything like the force it should command. Therefore the exhilaration of taking his first Church Service is often quickly checked. Though he is now at last doing what he has always longed to do, the whole thing may feel awkward, ineffective, and leave him very miserable. Hence the imperative necessity for technique. A man must not only *want* to preach; he must know *how* to preach.

Preaching is a high and difficult art which entails a long apprenticeship. On its human side the sermon is as much an artistic creation as a novel, a portrait, or a fugue. Admittedly the message is always greater than the way we utter it. Its result does not depend on our adhering to some literary or psychological formula. The simplest soul on earth may give a witness that has more life-changing energy than many masterpieces of pulpit eloquence. But to say that is merely to say that the Word of God cannot be bound. It is not to say that we should cease to study its effective presentation. Some folk have indeed considered it wrong to prepare religious discourses. These, they argue, should be left to the challenge of the moment and the aid of the Holy Spirit. But experience suggests that the Good News, far from being less free, is normally more dynamic and attractive when governed by the constraints of art. Life cannot endure for long on the basis of pure spontaneity. If it is to continue vital year after year it must operate within certain predetermined forms. So the business of technique is to make the most of what we have to say. By using a number of skilful devices we cause our utterance to march steadily and purposefully toward its goal. And we ought to be able to do this without the hearer knowing. True art conceals artistry.

Now almost every good sermon (however quickly put together in the end) has behind it a long history. Therefore our approach to the pulpit generally involves five distinct steps—gathering the material; fitting it into our plan; observing the homiletic laws; toiling to bring forth the message; and delivering it in the context of Public Worship. Let us look at these steps in that order. . . .

First, *GATHERING THE MATERIAL.* How does a sermon originate? Where does it come from? To a certain extent we are controlled in our choice by the demands of the Christian Year. So as we think forward to some particular week-end we may simply lift an appropriate text from one of the readings in the Lectionary. Which is a cold-blooded way of doing things and apt to carry its own low temperature into the pulpit. Few good sermons are manufactured. One does not just ' make ' them as one makes inanimate things. They have to be conceived, gestated, and brought to the birth. In Hebrews IV, 12, we read, ' The Word of God is alive.' Hence the content of scripture must never be treated as mere material. It is not débris on an excavation site to be discussed and ticketed by archæologists. It has the same present existence as we have ourselves. Therefore when it stirs within the mind we recognise it just as we would another individual who was addressing us. Every preacher knows the strange excitement which floods his breast when some seed-thought from the Gospel is over-shadowed by the Almighty. There is an unmistakable quickening. The word moves; it breathes; it cries aloud. And once generated like that it can seldom afterward be killed, even by the sorriest botch of a discourse.

Sermons must deal with Bible truth; but almost anything may furnish their starting-point—a wall-text, a stray remark, an incident in the news, a pastoral dilemma, an encounter on holiday, the sight of a tree against the moorland. What is important is not the exact nature of the stimulus but the receptive condition of the preacher himself. If he is required (as many are) to turn out two full sermons and three or four other addresses every week of his life, he cannot afford to wait until the hour is due before searching for a subject. That should be fixed beforehand. And the only way to make this possible is to have a 'bank of ideas' upon which he can draw. At first his capital in reserve will necessarily be small with the result that he is perhaps compelled to live a scrambling existence from week to week and may even begin to wonder how he can hope to sustain such an exhausting ministry. But as he gathers fresh riches and his investments begin to mature he should be able to plan for a much longer distance ahead.

The secret is for the preacher to become a new kind of person. He must acquire the homiletic mind. He must school himself to look at life always, as it were, from the pulpit. There is nothing reprehensible about that. It is an exact copy of the method which other men use who wish to be a success in their business or profession. A young student once spent a week-end in a district which is the centre of the Scottish lace industry. On the Monday morning one of the local manufacturers offered to drive him home. As they passed through the little towns and villages en route his host, motioning to the house-windows, kept up a running commentary, 'That's our Madras. . . . Yon's an old pattern now discarded. . . . These yellow fabrics have a special weave. . . .' and so on. Before the end of the journey the student realised that the manufacturer was 'curtain-conscious' to an extent of which he, who hardly noticed windows, had never even dreamed. Something of that same specialised outlook and concentrated vision should distinguish the preacher. As we gaze upon the world we ought to become 'sermon conscious.' We should see everywhere in our environment an opportunity of inducing men to consider life's eternal values and to close with the mercy of God in Jesus Christ.

Over and above the homiletic mind we need, if we can get it, the wealth of a book-lined study. What particular titles crowd the shelves depends upon the sort of person we are. But it is always a good omen when the largest group is concerned with the interpretation and exposition of the Bible. Even when we disagree with them they usually afford some afterglow of enlightenment. So one would counsel a beginner to spend his money not so much on books written by individuals (which can often be borrowed from libraries) as on standard works of reference. The more dictionaries, encyclopædias and concordances he has the better. They form the heart of any workshop and are worth yards of ephemeral theology. Let a man surround himself with solid tomes such as these and do his own digging. A proportion of other literature will, of course, be there also—recognised authorities in various fields, together with some volumes bearing on his specialised interests, and some which are frankly cultural or recreational. But what he must never forget is that his library has in the main a severely practical purpose. It does not require to be large; indeed it is in many ways better to be small; for it is not a retreat from the world but a sermon-creating background.

The next indispensable tool for a preacher is the cabinet or filing-system in which is stored away not only the results of his reading but also the whole product of his thought-life. Here is a hoard of assorted material—on the one hand study-notes, magazine articles, typed-out extracts, newspaper cuttings; on the other a vast array of sermon-drafts. This is the very core of the preacher's world. When Paul asked Timothy to bring him some things he had left at Troas, he added 'especially the manuscripts.' One's heart goes out to him there! What we have gathered in our files is indeed for our purpose above all earthly treasure. If administered aright it will go on continually growing in value. So not a day should pass but we slip some paper into it. There may be no obvious use for what we have culled or written just at that moment; but if it has 'sermonic quality' it should be laid up against a future need. Then once every two months or so a man may be well-advised to spend a leisurely morning fingering through his portfolios. If he does that he will discover that ideas apparently unrelated suddenly unite; and before long he has at the embryonic stage quite a number of new sermons.

These of course must ultimately be fitted into some kind of order; which brings us to our second main head —*THE PULPIT PLAN*. To preach just as vagrant impulse dicates is to give up any attempt at a balanced and fully-rounded ministry. How then are we to lay out our work? On what principle are subjects for the various Sundays to be chosen? Much will depend here on denominational practice and local circumstance. For those who are under obligation to follow a liturgy, the thing is easy; though that is far from saying that it is always religiously effective. But if we are not tied to a standard scheme, we must make one for ourselves.

Some believe in regular 'courses' of sermons. And doubtless that has its own value. Yet we can establish a unity in our work which is unbeholden to consecutive subjects. Much will depend on the nature of the man himself. There are those who think along serial lines; there are others whose habit of mind is occasional. An attempt should be made now and then to combine both patterns. But we ought not to allow a supposed necessity for chain-teaching of the scriptures to lead us too far away from our instinctive bent, still less to draw us into the marathon performance of preaching for months or years on the same book, which can be attempted only by a genius—and even then it is not always wise. After all, the pulpit is hardly the place for systematic instruction. That should be reserved in the main for the small groups and classes which supplement private Bible study. Any formal learning imparted by the preacher is purely incidental. The object of Public Worship is not to educate. It is to glorify God, and to establish that divine-human contact of which we have already spoken in a previous lecture.

One quite helpful way of planning forward is, near the end of June, to rough out an image of the next twelve-month as the preacher sees it. Calculation will show that he has to provide for about a hundred Services. He therefore takes two very large sheets of paper. On the first he draws up a list of all the sermon titles and any projected courses which he has at hand. On the second he outlines the Sundays of one complete year, and opposite each individual Sunday he puts a double or treble space according to the number of sermons it is going to require. Cancelling holidays, he then proceeds to mark off in red ink the great festivals, natural seasons, church anniversaries, celebrations of holy communion, youth parades, and other special diets. The next business is to take an appropriate sermon subject from sheet one and write it against its particular red-letter Sunday on sheet two. As these Sundays account on the average for almost half the total number, he is left with something like twenty-eight Sundays (i.e. fifty-six Services) which have no predetermined theme. Now begins the hardest part—arranging the unallocated opportunities so as to present in an orderly way successive aspects of the Gospel, and yet to keep up a steady contrast between the subjects dealt with morning and evening. A man is fortunate if he can win through even two thirds of this brain-racking job. Indeed in early years his resources may not stretch to more than a few weeks ahead. Nevertheless, the very making of the chart establishes a good habit and will amply repay his labour.

Of course it can be over-done. Too much of it tends to make a man a prisoner. And besides, life is not the neatly-ordered affair it sometimes seems from a manse study.

Allowance must be made for world changes and for invasive action by the Holy Spirit. We have also to recognise that ours is not just another earth-bound job. It shares in the paradox that runs through the whole of the Christian religion. If it be true that men should work according to schedule, it is equally true that there are hours when they must forget these office methods altogether. Every once in a while some heaven-sent message comes storming its way into the pulpit over the head of what we have prepared; and we must feel free to let it take possession of us. Then—his now irrelevant manuscript dashed from his fingers—the preacher speaks in burning words what God has at that very instant put into his mouth. One such 'flame day' will be recalled with awe and thanksgiving until the last of the generation that heard it is buried. Let us not despise prophesyings. For if we do, others will be raised up in our stead to speak to the people in 'Holy Ghost language.' A Church which began with the phenomena of the Upper Room can never be wholly rational.

But with that duly noted, we come back to our ordinary business. For as a general rule the danger lies not in too rigid adherence to a programme but in its very opposite, slack and dilatory workmanship. So if the message which we give on normal Sundays is to have artistic integrity, it must be composed with a certain regard for the principles of sermonising. And that leads us to our third main head—*OBSERVING THE HOMILETIC LAWS*. Every time we open our file, take out a given subject, and start on next Sunday's work, we should do so with certain rules in mind. Though the beginner is sharply aware of them, they tend by and by to become largely instinctive. Nevertheless, they are always mandatory. And even the most experienced preacher needs once in a while to recite them to himself again. If he has been losing grip, the chances are that he has either ignored or stupidly tried to disobey these wholesome canons. Let us look at a few of them now:

First, The Sermon-Theme Should Be Authoritative. That is to say, it should consist not of our individual observations about the Christian Faith but of some word which God has spoken or some truth He has revealed. There are men who use the pulpit to make their own comments from what they would describe as 'the Church point of view' on matters of general interest. They may do it with great ability; but that is not the purpose for which they were ordained. It brings their witness down to the level of journalism. Our message must rise above these trivialities. It should open up another world. And, furthermore, the manner of it should be strictly objective. Men come to church to hear from God—not from us. They do not want our views on bingo, or Moderator's hats, or nursing as a career, or atomic submarines, or the wickedness of South Africa's racial policy. What they do want is the one Word we are commissioned to speak. They can apply the New Testament teaching for themselves.

Again, The Sermon-Form Should Be Simple. There are of course some standard outlines, and we learn by experience which (if any) of these we should employ. But whether we choose the Three-Decker, the Spoked Wheel, the Graded Steps, or what-not, we must be careful. The shape of the sermon, though it decides how the message must be treated, has in itself no virtue unless we are willing to respect its particular constraints. If we disgorge material anyhow and anywhere we shall always land in chaos. We have only twenty minutes. So 'Prune! Prune! Prune!' is the preacher's watchword. Cut out all needless verbiage. Reduce the subject-matter to its essentials. Strive to be clear. Any fool can lose himself in a philosophic fog. It takes a first-class mind, great purity of heart, and much labour to achieve simplicity. Yet even if we can fulfil only the last-mentioned condition, the result will be well worth it.

Point three. The Sermon-Language should be Chaste. Unless a man walks very delicately his style of putting things may sometimes leave the saints pretty jangled. It is not so much *what* we say (for we have all the same body of truth to impart), it is rather *how* we say it that makes all the difference between our being found acceptable or otherwise. Language is therefore very important; far more so than the average minister believes. One single word can make or mar a whole discourse. Therefore even if we lack instinct enough always to hit upon the right expression, yet by study and care it is possible to avoid giving needless offence. Our message should be delivered in plain, sound Anglo-Saxon with a biblical echo. Forget the academic tongue. Avoid all slang, vulgarity and journalese.

Some hold that to talk in the language of the 'tabloid press' will establish bosom relations with the multitude. Quite the contrary. We are never more effective than when we are observing all the rules of good English.

Fourthly, The Sermon-Illustrations Should Be Few. A modest number is indeed necessary, but far more sermons have been killed *by* illustration than by the *want* of it; not because the illustrations were poor or awkwardly handled but simply because they were only illustrations. They did not have the force and authority of the Word itself. The man who, after he has used all that were genuinely required, sticks in two or three more because they are 'so apposite' is damping down the effect. His sermon grows weaker instead of stronger as he multiplies these ornaments. And, besides, there are some sources to which it is perhaps better that we should never go for this kind of material. One thinks of plays, novels, cinema films, and other works of the secular imagination. Striking and enjoyable as these may be, they carry no real weight with anyone who is in dead earnest about spiritual things; for in the last analysis they are, as the old Highland woman declared, 'chust a pack of lies.' Fiction may open up another world of ideas and motive, but it is fact we want in the pulpit; something which will bear the burden of man's immortal soul.

Fifthly, The Sermon-Substance Should Be Enriched with Quotations from The Bible. It is not enough to have a text. We should girdle it round with other illuminating passages. The Word interprets the Word. More than that, it has a sword-like quality. One of the first things a man discovers when he launches out on a Bible-based ministry is that God has now put into his hands a weapon far more powerful than he could hitherto have conceived. Why was he wasting his time with those ' life-situation ' sermons filled with extracts from every sort of literature except the Word of God? He even thought to change the human heart with bits from T. S. Eliot and flashes from Jean-Paul Sartre instead of the Gospel of the Son and His holy apostles. What blindness! What incredible folly! ' Scriptureless Preaching ' is a judgment brought on this present age by our own infidelity. Some who were trained in a theological school which scorned ' proof texts ' and looked upon the employment of Holy Writ almost as a sign of cultural barrenness are now deeply ashamed of their lack of facility there. They will never make it up in this life. But they utter a word of warning to the preachers of tomorrow. Know your Bible. Use your Bible. Prefer it far above all other books for the work you have to do. Quote it, and quote it again; not as men quote who have merely consulted a subject in the concordance but as those who are armed with a weapon that will do exploits for the Kingdom.

With these rules in mind, we come now in the fourth place to the crucial business of *TOILING TO BRING FORTH THE MESSAGE*. Let us suppose that the preacher has just entered one of those happy weeks (alas, so few in a busy charge) when the stream of calls and engagements is momentarily arrested and he can approach his main work with a certain leisure. He sits down at his desk. Before him is the Sunday morning subject, already verified in various commentaries. He chose it—or rather it chose him—originally because it was a ' living ' word; and he can still feel that primal excitement now. The idea, he discovers, has been fructifying in his mind. So out comes his pen and down go the queries, comments, insights and observations that have resulted. Then from his filing-system he gathers a certain amount of relevant material and a number of illustrations.

At this stage the whole enterprise requires a good deal of further thought before it can even begin to take shape. So after an hour or two he may leave it aside and turn to other things. If that afternoon (or on some subsequent day) as he makes his round of the invalids he can contrive to squeeze in an hour's walk, the very action of tramping along in meditation will carry the process a bit further. . . . Easily the most important thing he has to do is to arrive at a crystal-clear notion of his objective. What is this sermon intended to achieve? What truth does it declare? What hope can it give? What comfort will it bring? It is God's Word, authoritative, miraculous. It spoke to him when he first read it. This is his justification for noising it abroad. What will it say to the hearers? How is it going to affect their lives? . . . Back in his study again the preacher continues to worry away at sharpening the central statement. In the end, after many tries, he has fixed the title, and hammered out the heads. Now as the week draws on, he is ready to write.

One assumes that he will write his sermon. He need not read it. He may throw away the manuscript if he pleases. But there is a value in writing which is not otherwise to be secured. A man with a very logical head can lie on a couch and reason the whole thing through from beginning to end. But even so, unless he writes at least a portion of what he has excogitated, he will lose an indispensable training in exactitude and style. John Livingston who had a natural fluency trusted to it, with the consequence (as he regretfully admits) that he 'kept himself bare-handed all his days.' We ought to write. Some men start off with a blank sheet of paper, or only a few guide-words. Others make out a synopsis in more detail. It is generally an advantage to pay some attention to paragraphing. But whatever the method we decide to adopt once we have 'learned our trade,' nevertheless for a long stretch of the early years most of us should write. A man who dodges this discipline tends to inflict upon his congregation the worst effects of extempore speech. Much of the grace that should go with noble utterance is lost to him and to them for ever.

It is true that some of the greatest preachers, like George Whitefield, did not ordinarily write. It is also true that some of the greatest writers, like Sir Walter Scott, were hardly known to correct. But perhaps they would have been greater still in their respective spheres if they had submitted to the customary disciplines. Even Shakespeare marred his genius because (as Ben Jonson saw) ' he never blotted out a line.' Most of the really classic composition which has been done in this world was the issue of Sisyphean labour. One thinks, for example, of poems like Gray's ' Elegy ' or Lincoln's speech at Gettysburg. Even such a minor essayist as Virginia Woolf ' usually rewrote even the most ephemeral review seven times, with the result that the words seemed to be born from her pen . . . spontaneously . . . in a logical order of ideas.' Alfred Noyes admits that though his verses may appear to have been written *currente calamo*, sometimes there were ' at least a hundred drafts to produce a single easy-looking page or verse paragraph.' Francis Thompson's note-books tell the same tale. There we can observe how before he hit upon a magnificent line such as:

> Not where the wheeling systems darken . . . ,

he had already tried out the adjectives ' rolling,' ' hurtling,' ' whirling,' and ' rumbling '—just like the veriest amateur. Few things seem more straightforward in their childlike inevitability than Hans Andersen's fairy tales. Yet the manuscript that went to the printer was the end-result of a multitude of scorings, corrections, and re-arrangements—all in his own ' small spiky handwriting '—which shows that every word was weighed. Opening his heart to a friend, Joseph Conrad once confessed, ' I sit down for eight hours every day. . . . I write three sentences which I erase before leaving the table in despair. Sometimes it takes all my resolution to keep from butting my head against the wall.'

If that be the experience of those whose aim is bounded simply by literary concern, much more exhausting is the task that faces the preacher. For he has not only the difficulties of art to contend with; he has first a religious ordeal to undergo. Before heaven can speak through his lips he needs to be cleansed from the worldliness that has encroached upon his heart. Those third-rate standards by which men generally live must be swept away. As he has partly forgotten the 'Cross-Faith' he must return to it. Only by beating and battering the old self can he arrive at a genuinely spiritual outlook. There may even be some special sin which has repeatedly to be dealt with. Boston of Ettrick tells of the struggle he had with one of that type, and how he found comfort in the declaration, 'Such were some of you; but ye are washed, but ye are sanctified, but ye are justified. . . .' 'I walked up and down,' he says, ' with the Bible in my hand opened at that place, holding it up to heaven, as God's own word, pleading and improving it, for the cleansing of my vilest soul. . . . There I put all in Christ's hand.' There are times when we have to follow him in these passionate measures before we dare climb the pulpit steps again. So if ever the tyro supposed that sermon-making was easy, disillusionment awaits. He realises now that the business on which he is engaged is no mere fitting of certain ideas to their appropriate language but a harrowing of his very soul.

Then comes the hour when he must travail to bring forth the message. O that dreadful hour! What agony it is! Each of us tackles it in his own way, but every man is straitened to the limit. Some could tell of a preacher who forces himself to his desk; writes half a page; cancels most of it; buries his head in his hands; rises and walks the room; falls on his knees; goes back to the swivel chair; repeats the whole process; doggedly working away until at last the sentences begin to march and he thrills that the conflict is almost over. But every week, whatever his method, the preacher has to endure it again. There is no escape. Indeed, he gradually learns that there cannot be. This is the price of proclaiming the Word. Of course there are 'blinks,' sometimes quite extensive (just as there were in the Killing Time), when the torment is for a space remitted, but ordinarily a man has to go through with it. Blood and tears! Who can show us any other way? Yet there is virtue in the blood and converting grace in the tears. For what happens next Sunday will reflect (as has been said) 'with mathematical exactitude' his hours of hidden toil. In some mysterious fashion when he stands in the pulpit all the vital forces which he has poured out in this effort to know the mind of God will return upon him as an access of power from the Holy Spirit.

We come now in the fifth place to consider *THE HOUR OF DELIVERY*. The sermon is preached at Public Worship. It is the crowning act of a Service which contains various other elements. These are not there merely as a framework for the sermon. They exist in their own right. Nevertheless when carefully thought out beforehand they do greatly enhance the effect of the message. So as we climb the pulpit stair on a Sunday to begin the sacred exercise, we should have everything meticulously prepared. And because a seemingly trivial matter can ruin a whole Service, we must make sure that nothing within our own control is allowed to produce this melancholy result.

Hence these rules: Start the Service dead on time. Give out the hymns correctly. Have the Lessons plainly marked. Let the Intimations be typed in an orderly sequence. Study the banns of marriage. Be certain that you have grasped any new bit of ceremonial. Avoid desultory comment and sentimental embroideries. Announce each item according to the received formula —and only once; twice is to invite wandering of mind. Speak in a loud, clear tone, sustaining your sentences to the last. Finally, keep to the same length always. Public Worship is not the only engagement which our hearers have to fulfil.

Now as to the Service itself. Four things seem to call for special remark. First, *The Order of Worship*. Scholars hold different but often most dogmatic views about it. And indeed, most of us after exploring these mysteries have probably passed through a stage where the misplacement of a versicle or the omission of an epiclesis would have seemed nothing short of disaster. Fortunately the Holy Spirit is not as much exercised as we about such liturgical proprieties. The truth is that while some Orders of Service are more correct than others, almost any Order will do as long as the man who uses it is sincere.

Next, The Praise. Psalms and hymns must obviously be chosen according to some regulative principle. Whatever it is, it should govern both subject and form. This calls for thought. It cannot be done adequately on a week-to-week basis. So just as in the case of his sermons, the preacher should make out a praise-plan covering the Sundays of a whole year. It will need adjustment as circumstances change. But it ensures variety and guards against undue repetition. All Praise Lists should be communicated to the Organist at least some days (better a full week) prior to the Service, so that there is never any dishonourable scrambling at the last moment.

Then *The Prayers.* How are we to lead the congregation? Some adopt a purely extempore style which can be most effective. But the results are usually contra-indicated for a beginner. So he would be well-advised not only to write out some of his own prayers but also to draw freely upon the treasures stored up in Christendom's service-books. The idea that unless we pray always 'in our own tongue' we are guilty of dishonouring God is quite mistaken. When people have suffered under the vulgarisms and offensive particularities by which some earnest soul seeks to lead his flock to the throne of grace, they are often thankful thereafter to let their thoughts be carried along on the timeless language of the great ordinals.

The *Children's Address* is much frowned upon by purists. Perhaps not without reason. But for good or ill it has become an institution, and we must learn how to handle it. The danger is, of course, that it may break the unity of the Service. One way to prevent this is to make its subject the same as that of the sermon, so that it acts like a musical overture announcing the theme of the later work. It might be supposed that this was impossible, either because some adult concerns are not in the child's world or because of the difficulty of finding relevant material. But only academic subjects are really alien to the child. Those that come from the heart of the Bible generally speak to us irrespective of age. And material should present no difficulty. Almost always among the illustrations left over from the sermon there is one which can be used for this end. It had to be excluded as perhaps too long, too vivid, or too picaresque; but it is exactly right now. Thus the children's address far from interrupting the Service is made to underline and emphasise its message. . . . The remainder of the rules are these: One story only; a clear moral; never talk down; prepare every word; and keep within five minutes.

What of *The Sermon* itself? The moment we stand up to preach we have to decide our method. Are we going to read, to memorise, to use notes, or to launch out into spontaneous utterance? History can show samples of men who excelled in each of these different genres. Chalmers, Liddon, Stopford Brooke, all read. Boston, McCheyne, and Cyril Garbett memorised. F. W. Robertson, Kelman and Sangster worked from notes. Wesley, Spurgeon and William Temple were 'marvels of unpremeditated oratory.' The fact is that when these various styles are contrasted there is not a penny to choose between them. Each individual preacher must find out the way which is most natural to himself. It does not follow that because Dr So-and-So talks about the wonderful and rewarding adventure of schooling oneself to shut the Book and address the people face to face, we (if we try it) will necessarily share his exhilaration. Men are very differently constructed. In some the act of thinking interferes with the delivery of the message. They should read. In others the act of thinking is essential for the very production of the message. They should *not* read. Let each man pursue his own genius. The technique upon which he finally decides should be that which accords him the greatest spiritual liberty.

But when at last the hour arrives in which we have to proclaim the Word, nothing can really help us except the sense of communion with God. Great preaching is a mystery because although it involves the exercise of natural gifts its real strength lies in the enablement of heavenly forces. And we are not usually aware of them unless our whole life has been one long preparation for the pulpit. We cannot in a few scurried moments before the ordeal is due reverse the influences of a godless week. From Monday to Friday no less than at the week-end, we must walk with God. Saturday is the 'day of preparation' and should be kept as such. Rising in the Sunday quiet, while the world is yet asleep, we have time to say our prayers and review our task. Then we make for the House of God in sufficiency of time, holding extended discourse with no man by the way.

From the moment he announces his subject, a preacher should be oblivious of everything else except the faces of his hearers. Time is past now for technical considerations. He launches out in the enabling of the Holy Ghost. Indeed, he is no longer himself—only an instrument. Therefore as he warms to the work he may have the strange but quite definite sensation of being swept by an unseen power. His commonplace words are suddenly made to glow and throb with spiritual vitality. He feels with new nerve the heart-truth of his message. It burns in his own breast like a conflagration. So he urges it passionately, yet most tenderly, upon others. No one but the herald of God can describe the look of a congregation as worship mounts to its close; for then that mask which so many are accustomed to show to the world is stripped away. The preacher sees them in the nakedness of their soul—the shame, the penitence, the longing, the faith, the hope, the joy, the innermost of their immortal being. Who could remain unmoved by those eyes, gazing often out of the starkest human need into the infinite mercy of the Eternal? Here in the Church we have the answer to the sins and sorrow of our race. It lives in this Word which we are ordained to publish in the ears of men. Heaven forbid that we should ever think meanly of such an office, or of that holy creation—a true sermon—which may be used of God in bringing many sons unto glory. Let us go out to it then, every week, like Ebenezer

Brown, of whom the historian says, ' Six days he brooded over his message; was silent, withdrawn, self-involved . . .; on the Sabbath, that downcast, almost timid man . . . the instant he was in the pulpit, stood up like a son of thunder.' So may it be with all Thy servants, O Lord God Almighty!

V

PREACHER'S PILGRIMAGE

THE preacher inhabits a specifically religious world. His is the glorious privilege of handling holy things in the course of his daily business. Yet he must also walk as a man among men. Therefore his life-work, sacred though it is, does not miraculously preserve him from that element of corruption which still abides even in the regenerate heart. He too has a life to live and a death to die. He travels the same high-road as any ordinary member of the Christian Church. And the adventures which the saints have been accustomed to meet there will be his also. In one respect, however, his position is unique. As head of a journeying band it is his duty to set a good example. Above all others he should know how to keep his soul inviolate. 'Believe it brethren,' says Baxter, 'God never saved any man for being a preacher; but because he was a justified, sanctified man, and consequently faithful in his Master's work. Take heed, therefore, to yourselves . . . that you *be* what you persuade your hearers to *be*.'

The preacher's pilgrimage, when subjected to examination, will almost necessarily be found to include Some Ever-Present Dangers, Some Trustworthy Defences, and Some Life-Long Disciplines. We begin with *SOME EVER-PRESENT DANGERS. The first is often held to be Pride* —the original sin. But this, one ventures to hope, is a misjudgment. Few men in the ministry refuse to acknowledge their status as creatures. Most are sincerely desirous of acting as heralds of God. Their trouble is in general not pride but the lesser sin of vanity. Unlike the graduates of other learned professions, we are thrust straight away into a position of prominence which we have done little to merit. Dr Andrew Blackwood points out somewhere that almost everything about a young minister's life tends to make him conceited. And that is surely so. But the fact that we have been set over a congregation while it gives us authority 'to speak boldly in the name of the Lord Jesus' does not of itself endow us with those qualities of heart and mind which come only with the ripening of the years. When we start our life-work many of the folk who sit before us in church on a Sunday are old enough to be our parents—indeed, even our grand-parents. Now the Bible commands that we respect this difference in age. If we do so we shall be saved from the folly of 'preaching down' to our hearers. How sad a spectacle it is to see youth lecturing its father's generation on the business of living! People want us to be sure; not cock-sure. Scriptural teaching they will accept; but not jejune personal philosophy. So the rule for a beginner is: Stick to what you know. Publish revealed truth. Uphold sound doctrine. Bear your own testimony to Jesus Christ.

The passing of time should of course make us more lowly-minded. But self-importance is hard to eradicate. Our only real hope of remaining chastened in spirit is to gaze again at the Cross and see how the Lord of ten thousand worlds 'emptied himself' of all earthly dignities that he might minister to the very least of his brethren. 'I am among you as he that serveth.' 'Jesus knowing that the Father had given all things into his hand . . . took a towel. . . .' We are never safe unless we keep constantly in view the strange truth that in Christ's kingdom the qualification for the highest office is to be a slave. So, as not even the most modest of God's heralds is exempt from secret swellings of vanity, we must keep watch over the old nature. Fearing that he might become puffed up with the sight of thronging multitudes, Dr Billy Graham decided to open every one of his evangelistic campaigns in Britain with the chorus 'To God Be The Glory.' We also, though our sphere be much less in size than his, need the reminder that we are only instruments in the hands of the Eternal.

A second danger which threatens our pilgrimage is Worldliness. The ministry should be a vocation; but it is also to some extent a profession. This is because it has to be exercised in a visible church which, on one side, mirrors the organisational framework of other earthly societies. It is no use telling ourselves that we shall ignore the mundane element in the economy of God. We are only human. Men have always argued about place and power in the redeemed household. The Twelve did it. The Mediæval Curia did it. The Reformers did it. And even now nothing so excites a clerical gathering as to debate some change in stipend or the nomination of a particular candidate for a vacant office. If we think ourselves above these things we have little knowledge of our own heart.

Life is lived in periods each of which brings with it a new set of desires. Hence as he advances toward middle age a man may find within himself a hitherto unexperienced wish to stand well with the community —a hunger, indeed, for social recognition. He begins to crave as never before for greetings in the market-place. He likes to feel that his name is known and respected. And besides, while it is true that the Church does not hold out great monetary rewards, he also awakens to the fact that there are certain solid advantages to be gained from associating with the right people. . . . Now this attitude, if yielded to, breeds in a man an enthusiastic commitment to the values of this perishing order. He begins to judge even holy things by a material yardstick. The environment in which he then lives is one where no true thought of God ever enters. All the ideas possessing his mind are tinged with greed, envy, pride, excitement, competition. Moreover he quickly learns that if he is to ' get on ' in this power-world of the Church, he must speak smooth things and temper every absolute judgment lest he should antagonise somebody who might be useful afterwards.

Worldliness is a snare which the Christian preacher should avoid. We have renounced the vainglory of life. Even in the old Jewish Church the clergy were set apart. They had no real stake in the civil affairs of the nation. Their business was the House of God. ' The people of Israel,' we read, ' shall pitch their tents . . . every man by his standard; but the Levites shall encamp around the tabernacle of the testimony.' That is regulative still. It is not for us to be out where other men are, pursuing our private interests or going after the kind of success which involves striving and emulating. Our centre is the sanctuary. We are to abide by the altar of the Most High. In the apocryphal 'Gospel of Thomas' our Lord is reported to have said, 'If you do not fast to the world, you will not find the kingdom.' That rings true. It has always been true. Six hundred years ago Chaucer wrote of his Pourë Persoun:

> He settë nat his benefice to hyre
> And leet his sheepe encombred in the myre . . .
> He was a shepherde, and noght a mercenarie.

Four hundred years later Goldsmith said the same thing in his account of the Village Preacher:

> Unpractised he to fawn, or seek for power,
> By doctrines fashioned to the varying hour;
> Far other aims his heart had learned to prize. . . .

Even in the twentieth century the devoted herald keeps clear of material enticements that would steal away his heart. God will give us our daily bread; but relative poverty and actual obscurity are still, in the bulk of cases, by God's wise fore-ordaining, the faithful pastor's lot.

A third danger we have to face is Despondency. Perhaps if we fully grasped the wonder of our salvation we might always be filled with joy. But even the pilgrim who sets out with abounding gladness sometimes after a while begins to lose heart. He may, for example, be settled in a difficult charge. Congregations, like families, generate their own atmosphere. Some have always been unhappy. This may be due to an organisational fault such as a bad constitution. It is extraordinary how self-willed and obstructive otherwise good men can become when the law places in their keeping certain powers which they should never have had. Or it may be that there are a few awkward folk who constitute a lasting source of annoyance. Even one such can make a man's life a misery. It does not often happen that we have to cope with an open enemy, still less with a secret traitor. Yet such cases do arise. Even when our Lord Himself preached in Galilee there was a man present in church who 'had a devil.' And Paul also mentions certain trouble-makers who fell into the same category.

These personal strains tend to be felt most in our earlier years before we have learned how to handle the business side of a church. Later on, the thing which often gives us the sorest heart is the want of any clamant proof that ours has been a life-changing ministry. Not that the kirk has necessarily been ill-attended. Indeed we may have been accustomed to address a modest crowd Sunday by Sunday. But one can do that and still be weighed down by the suspicion—backed up perhaps by one or two grievous discoveries—that all the planning and praying and preaching seems to have gone for very little. This sense of having failed is a hard thing to bear. We read of others who have only to arrive in a parish or on a mission station for a work of grace to sweep through the whole district; and we are bewildered. Why should our harvest be so meagre?

Then there is the private side of our pilgrimage. A man may after a while begin to feel that the hour has come for making a fresh start in another sphere. All his guidance agrees. And yet when he begins to look around the prospect is sometimes rather discouraging. He tries; unsuccessfully. He tries again, with no better result. For the first time, perhaps, he learns how a person's whole future can hang on a casual incident; and how one word —and a false word at that—can shut the opening door. Or perhaps his age is the disqualification. To his astonishment he is made to realise that in the church a man, however competent and experienced, is often 'too old at forty.' Such a dashing of hope might be expected to leave a vacancy candidate embittered. In fact it seldom does so. But it may well trail behind it a memory of dark months and melancholy musings before the cloud is finally lifted.

Paul said the last word on this when he declared that though Christians might be downcast they were never destroyed. If we fall, it is only to rise again by the aid of God's Holy Spirit. A believer must be cheerful and of an equal mind in all conditions. Anything like lasting despair is a denial of the Faith. 'Great is their peace,' says William Penn, 'who know a limit to their ambitious minds; they have learned to be content with the appointments and bounds of Providence.' So for all men in the ministry who have dreamed of a charge without constitutional difficulties, or awkward members, or spiritual frustrations, there is comfort in the advice which John Newton once gave to a clerical friend who was wondering whether to go elsewhere, 'You know the whole of your present situation; of the other you can as yet know nothing. Your habits of life are adapted to Linkinhorne. . . . Where you are, you have been led on so gradually to preach the Gospel, that your people are now prepared, and know what to expect; in the other place you would have all to begin over again.' These are sound words. So we should leave the perfect parish where it belongs—in the world of fantasy; and address ourselves with a stout heart to the real job.

After these ever-present dangers that beset our pilgrimage, we come now in the second place to look at *SOME TRUSTWORTHY DEFENCES*. There are various things which can be reckoned on to uphold us in the work to which we are called. *First, for example, our Clerical Status*. Ordination is no mere formality tagged on at the end of our college years. It is a profound and life-changing experience, through which a man enters into a different world. Who can describe what happens in that awesome moment when he feels upon his head the magisterial hands of the Presbytery? Hitherto he had only intended holy orders. He may indeed have finished his theological course. He may have been licensed to preach. He may have worn the outward insignia of the sacred office. But he had not yet left the ranks of the laity. Now by this solemn rite his whole status is altered.

He becomes in the ancient sense of the word a 'clerk,' a religious person, a minister of Jesus Christ. Unless (which may heaven forbid!) he should by some unthinkable folly or scandal forfeit that status, it will belong to him until the day of his death.

Though we of the Reformed Church do not believe that ordination confers some magical grace, or that it cuts us off from the world in priestly seclusion, yet we do believe that it sets a man apart. That indeed is the very meaning of it. In title, purpose and function he now belongs to a different 'ordo'—a special group of Christians. This fact lays upon him a whole series of fresh responsibilities. He must learn a new way of life, the clerical vocation; just as a single person on marriage has to learn to be a spouse. All his conduct must be governed by the remembrance that he is a servant of the Church; one of its official and accredited representatives. Its honour is in his keeping. The carefree student days, when he expected others to take thought for him and his concerns, have vanished for ever. It is now his high privilege to pass from the company of those who receive to the company of those who give. Hitherto he has been ministered unto. Now he must minister.

If he is to do that, he ought from the very beginning to see clearly how he stands related to his fellows. One who wears clerical garb can never be an ordinary citizen. Therefore he is not as free as others are to form pleasant relationships of a private sort. Even if he dresses in mufti he cannot become just 'one of the boys.' And people know it. They are often a little discomfited by the back-slapping minister, even if politeness forbids them to tell. Ruskin said of the artist that ' He should be fit for the best society, and keep out of it.' That is our position also. Though the shepherd will care deeply for every member of his flock, he should think long before giving himself to individuals in the exclusive personal friendship which is natural elsewhere. For he has to maintain that priestly distance which enables him to speak to men as the herald of God, and on occasion to rebuke them for their sins. This he cannot so easily do if he has opened up the secrets of his life to them at fireside level. Hence the wise preacher will cut down purely social engagements to the minimum. People may want him as a friend—and, being human, he will almost certainly have a few intimates—but the bulk of his parishioners are better to know him as a soul-friend, the one appointed individual in the community whose lasting concern it is to keep them in the love and life of God.

If a man has an affectionate nature this question of status is likely sometimes almost to break his heart. The ministry is a lonely job. It cannot be otherwise. But when our flesh irks against these deprivations, we should remember that there is a blessed corollary. The very knowledge that we are ' set apart ' strengthens the soul and often enables us, as nothing else would, to overcome temptation. Arthur W. Hopkinson, once vicar of Banstead, describes in his autobiography how he was much troubled as to whether he should go on receiving generous gifts from a rich lady in his parish. In the end he got guidance to continue. But, he writes, 'I can thank God that as Juliet's priest and confessor, I never grew soft or remitted the tang of austerity in my affection for her.' That is the test. A man of that sort is safe anywhere. Quite incorruptible. And all because of the profound regard in which he held his ordination. If we can say 'For their sakes I sanctify myself' we shall not be left without our own meed of earthly friendship.

A second of our defences is Moral Consistency. Religion involves ethics. The Christian life works itself out in obedience to God's expressed will. Of course it must begin with a changed heart; but even so we have still to struggle with contrary desires. In other words, the experience of temptation and the daily effort to overcome it is necessary for anyone who is to grow in grace. Now a minister is not mysteriously exempt from this law. He has no inherent immunity from evil. And so he may find it much harder than he thought to stand up to the strains and stresses of the pastorate. Perhaps he did not quite realise when he entered the Church that every man there is fighting a battle; that the conflict is always a grievous thing; and all the more so because we are tested in secret and subtle ways through so much being left to our own sense of honour. We cannot afford to have a yawning gulf between precept and practice. Our words must be borne out by our deeds. 'Thou that teachest a man should not steal, dost thou steal? Thou that sayest a man should not commit adultery, dost thou commit adultery? Thou that abhorrest idols, dost thou commit sacrilege?' Paul's question to the typical Jewish rabbi carries even yet its blunt but necessary challenge to Christian ministers.

It is essential then right from the outset to give firm adherence to the moral law. We ought at intervals to ponder again the Ten Commandments and to reflect upon that instructive catalogue of the Seven Deadly Sins. More than other men we should show 'the ribbed and bony skeleton of righteousness' which validates our faith. People do not expect us to be paragons; but they do expect us to be consistent. John Stuart Mill once described the original members of the Oxford Movement as 'The first persons in England who for more than a century past have conscientiously and rigidly endeavoured to live up to what they normally profess.' We could not earn a better eulogium. This is what touches the outsider—the feeling that we already are what we are supposed to be. Can anyone show a more winsome advertisement for the Gospel than a life which is thoroughly good?

Hence we should seek in all things to stand morally above reproach. Our Father will richly repay those who are completely honest with Him, and who make an end of the shabby corners in their soul. The very fact that we have done so means that we have nothing now to dread. We can tackle life with a singing spirit. He who has a clean conscience has the secret of victory. He can go anywhere and take up any task. Like Sir Galahad, 'his strength is as the strength of ten because his heart is pure.' True, we shall never in this mortal life be perfect; but by renouncing every known sin and embracing the holy laws that lie behind the Gospel, we can become faithful servants of the Master.

Third in the list of our defences comes A Circumspect Walk. We are, of course, moral men; but in addition to that God requires that we should set an example to the believers. So the standard at which we aim must be above the average of the Christian community. It must in short be scrupulous and impeccable. Therefore we are obliged to think about the consequences of our slightest action. Everything we do is important, both in itself and also because of how it will appear to the onlooking multitude. Never are we at liberty to forget the hundreds of eyes turned upon us and the sharp brains that are being influenced by what they see. Even the manner in which we carry through an almost automatic performance like paying for a bus ticket can raise or lower the Church in the judgment of men. That is not to argue that we are therefore condemned to an unnatural existence. It is merely to affirm that people are right when they expect of us something elevated. Our life will derive from a heavenly source and have a touch of the austere.

This should be obvious in a number of ways. In our personal piety. A minister should need no injunction to kneel daily at the mercy-seat. It should be obvious in the eagerness with which we pursue our sacred studies. A lazy student will make a poor shepherd for any flock.

It should be obvious in our choice of a wife. We go against scripture if we allow ourselves to be yoked to a woman who whatever her other merits has no heart-interest in the Faith. It should be obvious in our home where family worship will be daily observed and children trained in Gospel manners. It should be obvious in our toilet. As far as we can make them so, the body and clothing of the Lord's servant should be clean, and his whole appearance well-groomed. It should be obvious in the reticence of our speech. No honourable man will gossip, or make wild charges, or use his people as illustrations for sermons and journalistic articles. It should be obvious in our handling of money. We shall pay our debts, live within our means, and in general wait until we can afford things before we proceed to enjoy them. It should be obvious in our dealings with the public. We cannot all have social gifts; but we can be so courteous, thoughtful, and appreciative that others will scarcely notice the lack; and we may even by these small graces persuade some who are still outside the Church to believe.

There are one or two further matters connected with our personal habits which demand consideration. Drink, for example. It is not often these days that a Scots minister uses alcoholic liquor regularly at his own table. But many, wishing to honour their host, or to identify themselves with the company, take a glass at public functions. That seemingly simple action raises an issue of the first magnitude. A minister who drinks thereby conveys the suggestion, especially to young folk, that this is both an innocuous and expedient thing for a Christian to do. The truth is that the beverage just taken into his hand has long since proved itself perhaps the single greatest curse of mankind. Thus he may ultimately be the cause of shocking damage to other people's lives. If he had left the thing alone he would have risked hurting no one; and he would have kept his moral authority unimpaired. Is there any doubt what a wise man should do?

Smoking is another issue that faces us. It has always been a dirty habit. But of recent years, with the widespread decline in manners, it has become a universal plague. People smoke everywhere. No place is too holy, no ceremony too sacred, to escape the fumes. The very House of God stinks with it. Is it too strong a use of language to call that 'an abomination'? Of course men persist in regarding it as a trivial matter, because they don't want to stop. But if ever they try, in nine cases out of ten they will find themselves fighting one of the supreme battles of their lives. Now there are some conflicts which a minister must win if he is to hold up his head as a spokesman of Jesus Christ. Can he worship the true God if he is already kneeling before an idol? Can he preach deliverance to the captives if he himself is a slave? Can he invoke health for the sick if, even as he prays, he may be busy undermining his own? When we have asked these questions we must judge in ourselves whether it be fitting that preachers of righteousness should still continue to indulge in a habit which even non-religious bodies almost unanimously condemn.

Having looked at some Ever-Present Dangers of our pilgrimage, and Some Trust-Worthy Defences, we come now to *SOME LIFE-LONG DISCIPLINES. First, Statutory Communion with God.* The heart of religion is fellowship with our Maker. Wonderful things happen to a man who is keeping his appointment in the secret place. His health improves. His work goes blessedly forward. Perhaps the only times in the ministry when we seem to be swept along on the wings of the Spirit and can hardly contain ourselves for joy are those when our devotional life is at a high level. But this ' euphoria ' may not endure. Dora Greenwell has pointed out that walking with God must always be for us (as it was for the Hebrews in the desert) a ' heavy, costly, sacrificing friendship.' Nobody can have it for long unless he is prepared to fulfil the requirements on which its continuance depends. And the trouble is that, after awhile, we tend to fall away.

Even the saints have never been able to understand why, though they experienced rapture at their orisons, they should then have been so unwilling to go back to God. That is an enigma which over-shadows us all. One might think that by the very force of our calling we should want to pray; indeed that we should be irresistibly impelled to pray. But how often we have had to drive ourselves to it! And how often this holy intercourse has been scamped or omitted! We remember days when we could hardly bear to enter our study because we should see at once the prie-dieu with the cushion lying before it, waiting for us to kneel. Yet that is the testing-point of our ministry. If we win through there, the heavens will open in blessing. If we let ourselves be defeated there, what have we to look forward to but an empty weary round; and at the last—judgment.

It is no use waiting for incentives to pray. Only fools expect some supernatural urge which will eliminate the ordinary human need for effort and agonising. There are no tricks by which we can achieve sainthood. It is the result of a certain way of life. Hence we must do with prayer what we have already done with preaching. It must be made a matter of discipline. Of course men vary so much in fitness, temperament, domestic obligations, and so forth, that one may well hesitate to lay down any general law. And in fact there is no need. The only essential thing is Regularity. We must pray as we eat our food, at more or less constant intervals. Yet though everybody's pattern may be slightly different, it is hard to challenge the assertion of John Henry Newman that, 'For morning and evening prayer all men can and should *make* leisure.' Dr. E. M. Blaiklock tells us why —'Prayer should be the key of the day and the lock of the night.' To these salutory dicta the Psalmist would add a third, 'Evening and morning, *and at noon,* will I pray.' That seems the perfect arrangement.

True, a man whose mind is most active after the rest of the world has sought its pillow will be tempted to postpone his chief devotional office until the small hours. But if there is no unavoidable cause why this must be so, it is worth a big fight to reverse the order. The night shift has never in any job been quite as natural or wholesome as the day shift. It is good to meet with our Maker in the freshness of the dawn. Private prayer before breakfast is the traditional mode in Christian households; and it does not seem likely that we can improve upon it. . . . Then without waiting for the actual stroke of noon, we can cultivate the habit of talking with God, just under our breath, at almost any moment of the day—thanking Him for a vase of flowers, asking His help about an awkward visit, glorifying His name for some echo of revival, and so on. It was said of Spurgeon that he was seldom found on his knees because his entire life was really a conversation with the Most High. There is a danger in that, but a lesson too. Our stated prayers will have more intimacy, and perhaps more reality, if we have been darting little messages to our Father from sunrise to sunset. . . . The evening is a good time at which to hold intercessions for the sick. Though the mind may by then be somewhat jaded, the very fact that we are praying for people whose faces we now visualise is a splendid aid to concentration. Indeed that ' sanctuary hour ' can become one of the most blessed aspects of our ministry. It sends us to bed at night with a new glow of faith, as well as with the happy consciousness that while we sleep God will be calming fevered thoughts, healing broken bodies and generally continuing His mighty work of grace.

A second discipline which we are in duty bound to undergo is The Maintenance of our Personal Efficiency. God has a right to expect that we shall at all times bring to His work the utmost we can give. Therefore we must take care of our Health. The ministry is an exacting job. Of recent years there has been a marked increase in the number of men breaking down in their forties or fifties. Some at least of these disasters are preventable. We cannot indeed change the whole tempo and character of the modern world. But we can resolve to live an orderly existence. Constantly changing meal-times (due to funerals, marriages, and the like) is one of our most intractable problems. There is little we can do about that. But want of exercise—a common failing with motorists—is easily curable. A man should dig in his garden, or take a country walk, or otherwise open up his lungs, as regularly as he says his prayers. The flesh needs it. And as most people eat too much, why overlook the fact that fasting has scriptural authority? It was practised by our Lord. Some of us have found it, just as He did, an invaluable aid to the spiritual life.

After health comes what one can only call Stream-Lining. That is to say, if we are to concentrate on the main things, our work must be smoothed down to its essentials and all unnecessary effort eliminated. A young man in his first charge sometimes thinks himself obliged to reach an ideal standard of excellence. But the only result of attempting it—apart from a prodigal waste of energy—is frustration and weariness. We can never do all we are supposed to do. We cannot answer every request. We cannot speak at every meeting. We must choose. And besides, the men who serve God in His Church are not all of the same type. On the contrary, they are infinitely varied—in gift, in brain-power, in natural vitality. There are things which each one can do, and things he cannot do. The fact that others can do these same things quite easily is irrelevant. We must respect our limitations. Therefore unless we are to lose control of our life altogether we shall be wise to follow Spurgeon's counsel, 'Learn to say "No." It will be of more use to you than to be able to read Latin.' Such an attitude is bound, of course, to make us enemies. But, after all, that is the price of being really effective in one's own vineyard.

Another indispensable aid to efficiency is the Rest Period. This may take one of several forms. God has ordained for us sabbaths and jubilees. Many a preacher forgets that as the normal 'day of rest' is for him the busiest of all, he is under solemn obligation to keep the spirit of the commandment by observing another. If we do not arrange (as far as circumstances allow) to have a whole day off each week, we shall soon feel spiritually jaded. That is the minimum we need for worship, for the cultivation of family life, and for the relaxing of mind and body. . . . Holidays are another illustration of the same principle. Grudge no money spent on them; and ignore the small-minded folk who because of their ignorance think that a minister can be made as good as new by an occasional week-end at the sea-side. One month in summer is all too short. The great Victorians took two. Many American churches give their preacher a roving commission every seventh year. And certainly if we can contrive to go abroad, that will extend our outlook and immeasurably enrich our thoughts. How wonderful to have stood by the lake-shore of Galilee; to have gazed at the ruined splendours of Greece and Rome; and to have some acquaintance with the towering cities and teeming peoples of the Modern World! . . . Besides that, we should now and then leave home to make a spiritual retreat. It can be a purely personal thing; or it may take us into a company of devout souls who thirst, even as we do, for a fuller knowledge of the Lord. Conversion is not enough. We need from time to time to pledge ourselves once more. Happy the man who, as he thinks of these memorable hours can echo the feelings of Thomas Boston, 'I had some Bethels, where I met with God, the remembrance whereof hath many times been useful and refreshful to me, particularly a place under a tree in Kennet orchard, where, Jan. 21, 1697, I vowed the vow, and anointed the pillar.'

A third of these life-long disciplines is The Shepherding of The Flock. Ours is essentially a pastoral ministry. It involves a close and lasting bond between preacher and people. They are his charges. Therefore he cannot just rise and go off at any moment to satisfy some personal whim. Even holidays need to be organised well in advance. He is tied to his flock as a mother to her child.

They are no mere occasional interest or spare-time occupation. They are his life. Indeed one of the darkest shadows that ever crosses his mind is the thought that one day, perhaps, while he is still in this world, he may have to leave them. Meanwhile they are his constant and absorbing care. He prays for them. He counsels with them. He visits them in their homes. His every message is composed with this particular auditory in view. And for a very good reason. These people are in fact (under God) largely dependent on him for the vitality of their spiritual life. They themselves acknowledge it. They look forward to the Sabbath and hunger for the Word.

Now there are certain critics who regard this as a perverted state of affairs. The Church, they argue, was never meant to be an in-turned group rejoicing in its own warm sodality. It should go out to evangelise. That of course we allow. But need the two things be mutually exclusive? Family fellowship must surely exist before we can have any evangelical out-reach. The trouble is that too often in the immediate past we have been inclined to think of the Church as an absolutely Christian household from which to send missionaries to an utterly pagan world. But that is hardly realistic. This is not the first century. The Church has now permeated the world—but, alas, the world has also to some extent permeated the Church. Hence in any so-called 'Christian' land today, the Church itself is the biggest and most promising mission field.

It follows that no parish minister need apologise for

giving the main bulk of his time to his own congregation. If he ventures out into the highways and hedges he merely lands in his neighbour's territory, where he ought not to be. Let him stay at home and dedicate his life to the task God has put into his hand. Every person he wins for Jesus Christ is a potential evangelist. So ultimately the influence he exerts will extend far beyond his own borders. And thus the Kingdom will come. But this needs all his mettle. How easy it is to fritter away our strength on small and perfunctory things, mere clerical trivialities, while the great business of the Church is left to languish! In his private diary young Jonathan Edwards wrote, 'Frequently, in my pursuits of any kind, let this question come into my mind, "How much shall I value this upon my death-bed?"' That gives the true perspective for the Christian ministry. It sends a man up to the pulpit with a burden which he must discharge. He is to love these people. He is to instruct them, challenge them, appeal to them until they yield their hearts and are established in righteousness. Each is a precious soul for whose everlasting welfare he will be called to account at the mercy seat. The late Archbishop of York used to say to his young men on the eve of their ordination to the priesthood, 'Tomorrow you will stand before me, and I shall ask you, "Will you . . . ? Will you . . . ? Will you . . . ?" One day you must stand before the Lord Who will ask, "Have you . . . ? Have you . . . ? Have you . . . ?"' That is indeed the ultimate interrogation. And there is probably not one of us who does not tremble as he thinks of it. But how reassuring it will be if we find others there—others who, with the remembrance of the work we did on earth, can give loving support to our own faltering testimony!

> Oh! If one soul from Anwoth
>   Meet me at God's right hand,
> My Heaven will be two Heavens,
>   In Immanuel's land!

INDEX

SCRIPTURE REFERENCES